LONDON AND MI

A GENEALOGICAL BIBI

Volume 2
Family Histories and Pedigrees
Second edition

By
Stuart A. Raymond

Published by the
Federation of Family History Societies (Publications) Ltd,
The Benson Room, Birmingham & Midland Institute,
Margaret Street, Birmingham, B3 3BS, England

Copies also obtainable from:

S.A. & M.J. Raymond, 6, Russet Avenue, Exeter, EX1 3QB, U.K.

First published 1994
Second edition 1997

ISBN 1-86006-059-5

ISSN 1033-2065

Printed and bound by The Alden Group, Oxford OX2 0EF

Contents

Introduction

This bibliography is intended primarily for genealogists. It is, however, hoped that it will also prove useful to historians, librarians, archivists, research students, and anyone else interested in the history of London and Middlesex. It is intended to be used in conjunction with my *English genealogy: an introductory bibliography,* and the other volumes in the *British genealogical bibliographies* series. A full list of these volumes currently available appears on the back cover.

Published sourcs of information on the capital's genealogy are listed in volume 1 of the present work; this volume lists works devoted to specific families, together with collections of pedigrees, biographical dictionaries, diaries, and works on heraldry and surnames. It includes published books and journal articles, but excludes the innumerable notes and queries found in family history society journals and similar publications, except where the content is of importance. Where I have included such notes, replies to them are cited in the form 'see also', with no reference to the names of respondents. I have also excluded works which have not been published. Where possible, citations indicate the period covered, the locality/ies in which the families concerned dwelt, and other pertinent information.

Be warned: just because information has been published, it does not necessarily follow that it is accurate. I have not made any judgement on the accuracy of most works listed: that is up to you.

This bibliography deals with works concerning the historic City of London and County of Middlesex, as they were prior to the nineteenth century. London has, of course, expanded greatly into the surrounding counties, and the former Greater London Council took in large chunks of Kent, Surrey and Essex. These areas are or will be dealt with in the volumes to be devoted to those counties in the *British Genealogical Bibliographies* series.

Anyone who tries to compile a totally comprehensive bibliography of London and Middlesex is likely to fall short of his aim. The task is almost impossible, especially if the endeavour is made by one person. That does not, however, mean that the attempt should not be made. Usefulness, rather than comprehensiveness, has been my prime aim — and this book would not be useful to anyone if its publication were to be prevented by a vain attempt to ensure total comprehensiveness. I have been able to add more than 100 additional family histories for this edition; nevertheless, I am well aware that there are still likely to be omissions, especially in view of the fact that, given constraints of time and money, it has not been possible for me to check the holdings of all the fifty or more libraries and record offices with substantial collections on London's history. Each of them may well possess works not held anywhere else. The identification of such works is not, however, a major aim of this bibliography. Rather, my purpose has been to enable you to identify works which are mostly readily available, and which can be borrowed via the inter-library loan network irrespective of whether you live in London or Melbourne. Most public libraries are able to tap into this network; your local library should be able to borrow most items I have listed, even if it has to go overseas to obtain them. Space prohibits a listing of London local studies collections, but a number of guides to them are listed in volume 1.

If you are an assiduous researcher, you may well come across items I have missed. If you do, please let me know, so that they can be included in the next edition.

The work of compiling this bibliography has depended heavily on the resources of the libraries I have used. A full list of these cannot be given; however, they included Exeter University Library, Exeter Central Library, the British Library, the Society of Genealogists, Guildhall Library, the Bishopsgate Institute, Greater London History Library, and the local studies libraries at Hounslow, Uxbridge, Swiss Cottage and Victoria. I am grateful to the librarians of all these institutions for their help. For this second edition, I have had the advantage of being able to check my listings against Heather Creaton's massive *Bibliography of published works on London history to 1939,* which appeared too late to be checked for the first edition. I am grateful too to all who have written to me with suggestions for inclusion. Mionie Dryden corrected my typescript, and Bob Boyd saw the book through the press. The support of the officers of the Federation of Family History Societies is, of course, vital for the continuation of this series. My thanks also to my wife Marjorie and to my children, who have lived with the *British genealogical bibliographies* for some seven years now.

Stuart A. Raymond

Bibliographic Presentation

Authors' names are in SMALL CAPITALS. Book and journal titles are in *italics.* Articles appearing in journals, and material such as parish register transcripts, forming only part of books are in inverted commas and textface type. Volume numbers are in **bold** and the individual number of the journal may be shown in parentheses. These are normally followed by the place of publication (except where this is London, which is omitted), the name of the publisher and the date of publication. In the case of articles, further figures indicate page numbers.

Abbreviations

B.T.L.H.S.	Borough of Twickenham Local History Society
C.A.	Cockney ancestor
C.H.R.	*Camden history review*
C.T.G.	*Collectanea topographica et genealogica*
E.H.H.S.	Edmonton Hundred Historical Society
Gl.M.	*Guildhall miscellany*
H.F.H.S.M.	*Hillingdon Family History Society magazine*
J.H.H.L.H.S.	*Journal of the Hayes and Harlington Local History Society*
J.S.S.L.H.S.	*Journal of the Sunbury and Shepperton Local History Society*
L.R.	*London recusant*
M.G.H.	*Miscellanea genealogica et heraldica*
N.E.H.G.R.	*New England historical and genealogical register*
N.M.	*The North Middlesex: journal of the North Middlesex Family History Society*
N.S.	New series
Pr.Hug.Soc.L.	*Proceedings of the Huguenot Society of London*
R.N.E.	*Ruislip, Northwood & Eastcote Local History Society journal*
T.L.M.A.S.	*Transactions of the London and Middlesex Archaeological Society*
U.R.	Uxbridge record
W.D.D.H.	*West Drayton and District historian*
W.H.S.J.	*Wembley History Society journal*
W.M.	*West Middlesex Family History Society journal*

1. GENEALOGICAL DIRECTORIES

A. Genealogical directories

One of the first things to do when tracing your family tree is to make contact with others researching the same name. They may have already done all the work! A number of national directories of genealogists' interests are listed in Stuart Raymond's *English genealogy: a bibliography,* section 7. The local offshoot of one of these is:
British Isles genealogical register: Middlesex and London. 3 fiche. 2nd ed. Birmingham: Federation of Family History Societies, 1997.
The various local family history societies have also published directories of their members' interests. See:
MOORE, EILEEN D. *The London and Middlesex genealogical directory.* Ilford: Association of London and Middlesex Family History Societies, 1980. Now rather out of date, but could still be useful.

Central Middlesex
CENTRAL MIDDLESEX FAMILY HISTORY SOCIETY. *Members interests.* The Society, 1988.

East of London
BUNTING, JEANNE. *Members interest directory, 1991.* East of London F.H.S., 1991.

Hillingdon
HILLINGDON FAMILY HISTORY SOCIETY. *Directory of members interests.* Hillingdon Family History Society, 1997.

London and North Middlesex
LONDON AND NORTH MIDDLESEX FAMILY HISTORY SOCIETY. *Directory of members' interests 1990-1994.* 1 fiche. The Society, 1994.

West Middlesex
WEST MIDDLESEX FAMILY HISTORY SOCIETY. *Member's surname index.* 1 fiche. The Society, 1993.

2. NAMES

The medieval origins of London surnames are discussed in a number of works by Eilert Ekwall:
EKWALL, EILERT. *Early London personal names.* Lund: C.W.K. Gleerup, 1947. To the 12th c.
EKWALL, EILERT. *Studies on the population of medieval London.* Stockholm: Almqvist & Wiksell, 1956. Suggests the origins of many surnames amongst migrants from the Midlands.
EKWALL, EILERT. 'Variations in surnames in medieval London', *Arsberättelse: Bulletin de la Société Royale des Lettres de Lund* **1944-5,** 207-62.
See also:
MCCLURE, P.T 'Patterns of migration in the late middle ages: the evidence of English place-name surnames', *Economic history review* 2nd series **32,** 1979, 167-82. Analysis of surnames in Nottinghamshire, Leicester, Nottingham, Norwich, York and London.
RUSSELL, JOSIAH C. 'Medieval midland and northern migration to London, 1100-1365', *Speculum* **34,** 1959, 641-5.

3. BIOGRAPHICAL DICTIONARIES, ETC.

Biographical dictionaries provide much useful information on their subjects. All of those listed in *English genealogy: a bibliography,* section 7, include Londoners amongst their subjects. A number of dictionaries published in the late nineteenth/early twentieth centuries deal specifically with Londoners, and are listed here (in chronological order).

PRESS, C.A.M. *Middlesex men of mark: a portrait gallery.* Jarrold, 1894.

Leading men of London: a collection of biographical sketches. British Biographical Co., 1895.

WELCH, CHARLES. *London at the opening of the twentieth century.* Brighton: W.T. Pike & Co., 1905. This volume includes PIKE, W.T. *Contemporary biographies,* which has been reprinted in WELCH, C. *A dictionary of Edwardian biography. London.* Edinburgh: Peter Bell, 1987.

[NORTH, ALLAN.] *Middlesex: biographical and pictorial.* Saltmarsh: Allan North, 1906.

London leaders, historic families, ancestral estates. Allan North, 1907.

Prominent men of London: a collection of portraits of men who ... have attained distinction in the premier city of the world: London. Shaftesbury Press, 1907-9. Portraits only.

Notable Londoners: an illustrated who's who of professional and business men. 6 vols. London Pub. Agency, 1922-8. Title varies: alternatives are *The illustrated who's who* and *Notable personalities.*

KENT, WILLIAM. *London worthies.* Phoenix House, 1949.

Much information of a biographical nature is to be found in works dealing with the homes of famous residents, and with London statues. Many such works are available; the following titles are representative of their genré.

BURROWS, VICTOR, ed. *The blue plaque guide to historic London houses and the lives of their famous residents.* Newman Neame, 1953. Effectively a biographical dictionary.

HALL, MARTIN. *The blue plaque guide to London homes.* Queen Anne Press, 1976.

BAKER, MARGARET. *London statues and monuments.* 3rd ed. Shire Publications, 1992. Includes biographical notes.

BLACKWOOD, JOHN. *London's immortals: the complete outdoor commemorative statues.* Savoy Press, 1989. Includes biographical notes.

BYRON, ARTHUR. *London statues: a guide to London's outdoor statues and sculpture.* Constable, 1981. Includes biographical notes.

COOPER, C.S. *The outdoor monuments of London: statues, memorial buildings, tablets and war memorials.* Homeland Association, 1928. Includes much biographical information on persons commemorated.

4. PEDIGREE COLLECTIONS AND HERALDRY

A. *Pedigree collections*

The modern genealogist is fortunate in being able to draw on the labours of earlier workers in the field. A number of pedigree collections listed in Raymond's *English Genealogy: a bibliography,* section 7, include London pedigrees, and should be consulted. Amongst the earliest genealogists were the heralds of the sixteenth and seventeenth centuries, who regularly conducted 'visitations' of the counties in order to determine the right of gentry to bear arms. This involved the compilation of pedigrees. Many of these visitation pedigrees have been published — although frequently in a corrupt form. For London and Middlesex, see:

RAWLINS, SOPHIA, ed. *Visitation of London, 1568, with additional pedigrees, 1569-90, the arms of the City companies, and a London subsidy roll, 1589,* transcribed and annotated by H. Stanford London. Publications of the Harleian Society **109-10,** 1963. This partially supersedes:

HOWARD, JOSEPH JACKSON, & ARMYTAGE, GEORGE JOHN, eds. *The visitation of London in the year 1568, taken by Robert Cooke, Clarenceux King of Arms, and since augmented both with descents and arms.* Publications of the Harleian Society **1.** 1869. For a critical review, see *Herald and Genealogist* **6,** 1871, 440-8. This began to be printed as a supplement to *L.M.A.S.* in 1861. However, only one small part was actually published in this form, covering the families of Chester, Martyn, Champion and White only. The whole visitation was subsequently published by the Harleian Society in the volume cited.

HOWARD, JOSEPH JACKSON, & CHESTER, JOSEPH LEMUEL, eds. *The visitation of London, anno domini 1633, 1634 and 1635, made by Sr. Henry St.George, Kt., Richmond Herald, and deputy and marshal to Sr. Richard St.George, Kt., Clarencieux King of Armes.* 2 vols. Publications of the Harleian Society **15 & 17,** 1880-83.
'Pedigrees from the visitation of London, 1633-34', *M.G.H.* **1,** 1868, 50-53 & 280-83.

Pedigrees include Hobson, Norton, Cowper, Smith, Ofspring, Martin, Leman, Sainthill, Newby, De La Barr and Foxcroft.

FOSTER, JOSEPH, ed. *The visitation of Middlesex began in the year 1663, by William Ryley, esq., Lancaster, and Henry Dethick, Rouge Croix, marshalls and deputies to Sir Edward Bysshe, Clarencieux, as recorded in the College of Arms (D.17).* The author, 1887. This supersedes:

[PHILLIPPS, T., SIR], ed. *The visitation of Middlesex began in the year 1663 by William Ryley, esq., Lancaster, and Henry Dethick, Rouge Croix, marshals and deputies to Sir Edward Bysshe, knt, Clarencieux King of Arms.* J. Nichols, 1820.

WHITMORE, J.B, & CLARKE, A.W.H., eds. *London visitation pedigrees 1664.* Publications of the Harleian Society **92.** 1940.
'Some pedigrees and arms from the visitations of London, 1664 and 1687', *M.G.H.* 5th series **8,** 1932-4, 22-8, 54-5, 76-8, 125-6, 158-9, 182-91, 224-8, 239-46, 277-81, 305-9 & 341-9. These pedigrees are fully listed in Raymond's *British genealogical periodicals* vol.3(1), 44.

In addition to the Heralds' visitation returns, a number of other pedigree collections are available in print:

ARMYTAGE, GEORGE JOHN, SIR, ed. *Middlesex pedigrees as collected by Richard Mundy in Harleian ms. no.1551.* Publications of the Harleian Society **65,** 1914.

CLARKE, A.W.H. *London pedigrees and coats of arms.* M.Hughes and Clarke, 1935. Reprinted from *M.G.H.*
'London pedigrees and coats of arms from Add.ms.5533 and Harl.ms.1096', *M.G.H.* 5th series **2-7,** 1916-31, *passim.* These pedigrees are fully listed in Raymond's *British Genealogical periodicals* vol.3(1), 43-4.

Many Chelsea pedigrees are printed in:

DAVIES, RANDALL. *Chelsea Old Church.* Duckworth & Co., 1904. This also includes monumental inscriptions, and notes on the parish register (including extracts).

Huguenot pedigrees available at the French Hospital are listed in:
'Pedigrees of Huguenot families and materials compiled and collected by Henry Wagner, F.S.A.', *Pr.Hug.Soc.L.* **13**, 1923-9, 287-95.
A list of gentry in 1673 is given in:
'London and Middlesex gentry in 1673', in PHILLIMORE, W.P.W. *The London & Middlesex notebook.* Elliot Stock, 1892, 74-6, 118-24 & 166-70.
For pedigrees of particular families, see section 6.

B. Heraldry

A number of armorials are printed in the Royal Commission on Historical Monuments' *Inventories*:

ROYAL COMMISSION ON HISTORICAL MONUMENTS (ENGLAND). *An inventory of the historical monuments in London.* 5 vols. H.M.S.O., 1924-30. v.1. Westminster Abbey (includes armorial). v.2. West London. v.3. Roman London. v.4. The City (includes armorial). v.5. East London (includes notes on brasses and heraldry).

ROYAL COMMISSION ON HISTORICAL MONUMENTS (ENGLAND). *An inventory of the historic monuments in Middlesex.* H.M.S.O., 1937. Includes armorial of heraldry, before 1550.

Much heraldic information on London families has been published, especially in the columns of the *Miscellanea genealogica et heraldica (M.G.H.)* This includes grants of arms, funeral certificates, heraldic bookplates, *etc.* The following list includes many brief notes on particular families and individuals.

Abbot
C[OKAYNE], G.E. 'Funeral certificate of Dame Margaret Abbot', in PHILLIMORE, W.P.W., ed. *The London & Middlesex notebook.* Elliot Stock, 1892, 41-3. See also 83-4. 1630.

Allen
See Robarts

Aylmer
'Funeral certificates: John Aylmer, Bishop of London, 1596', *M.G.H.* N.S. **4**, 1884, 154-5.

Baker
GATFIELD, GEORGE. 'Confirmation of arms and crest to George Baker of London, gentleman, 1573', *Genealogist* N.S. **6**, 1890, 242.
'Confirmation of arms, by Robert Cooke, Clarenceaux, to George Baker of London, gentleman, 1573', *M.G.H.* **2**, 1876, 1-2.
'Grant of arms by Sir Thomas St.George, Garter, and Sir Henry St.George, Clarenceux, to John Baker of the City of London', *M.G.H.* 3rd series **2**, 1898, 65. 1702.

Bayliff
BAYLIFFE, C. MEREWETHER. 'Confirmation of arms and grant of crest to John Bayliff', *M.G.H.* N.S. **28**, 1906, 152. 1623.

Beckett
'Grant of arms to Oliver Beckett of Queen Square, esquire', *M.G.H.* N.S. **2**, 1877, 192.

Bentley
'Grant of arms to Edward Bentley of Ely Place, 1838', *M.G.H.* N.S. **3**, 1880, 122.

Blackburn
'Confirmation of arms and grant of crest to John Blackburn of London, 1784', *M.G.H.* 5th series **3**, 1918-19, 86.

Blackmore
'Grant of arms by Sir Edward Bysshe, Clarenceux, to John Blackmore of London, 1661', *M.G.H.* 2nd series **3**, 1890, 269(f). Facsimile.

Bowes
EVANS, C.F.H. 'The arms of Sir Martin Bowes, Lord Mayor of London, and his wives', *Coat of arms* **7**, 1962-3, 153-6. 16th c.

Broad
'Grant of arms to Henry Broad of Chiswick', *M.G.H.* N.S. **2**, 1877, 311. 1637.

Brock
'Exemplification of arms and grant of crest, by William Camden, Clarenceux, to William Brock, of the Inner Temple, esquire, 1602', *M.G.H.* **2**, 1876, 17-18.

Brown
'Grant of arms to James Brown, 1789', *Genealogist* **1**, 1877, 220-21.

Burfoot
'Confirmation of arms and grant of crest to Thomas Burfoot of London, 1752', *M.G.H.* 2nd series **3**, 1890, 397.

Cambell
FLETCHER, W.G.D. 'Exemplification of arms and crest to Thomas Cambell esquire, citizen and alderman of London, 20 September, 42 Elizabeth, 1600', *Genealogist* N.S. **21**, 1905, 187-8.

Chitwood
'Funeral certificate: Sir Roger Chitwood, 1635', *M.G.H.* 2nd series **1**, 1886, 122.

Clayton
'Bookplate of Sir Robert Clayton', *M.G.H.* 3rd series **1**, 1896, 137. 17th c.

Cokayne
COKAYNE, G.E. 'Funeral certificate of William Cokayne, esq., of London, 1599', *M.G.H.* 2nd series **4**, 104-5. Also of Sir William Cokayne, 1626.
'Cokayne: [blazon and exemplification of arms to William Cokayne the eldest, and to his seven sons] 10 October 1597', *M.G.H.* N.S. 3rd series **3**, 1900, 261-7. Of Derbyshire and London; includes abstracts of medieval deeds.

Davidson
'Confirmation of arms and grant of crest, by William Cooke, Clarenceux, to William Davidson of London, gentleman, 1575', *M.G.H.* **1**, 1868, 273-4.

Dawes
'Funeral certificate: Sir Jonathan Dawes, Kt., 1672', *M.G.H.* 2nd series **4**, 1892, 145.

Decker
'Confirmation of arms to Sir Mathew Decker of the City of London, 1716', *M.G.H.* 2nd series **4**, 1892, 289-90.

Dicer
BURKE, H. FARNHAM. 'Funeral certificate: Sir Robert Dicer, Baronet, 1667', *M.G.H.* 3rd series **4**, 1902, 189. Of Hackney.

Draper
'Grant of arms and crest to Henry Draper, of Colbrooke, Middlesex, 1571', *M.G.H.* 3rd series **4**, 1902, 169.

Eldred
'Confirmation of arms and grant of crest to John Eldred of London', *M.G.H.* 5th series **7**, 1929-31, 308.

Elken
'Grant of arms and crest to Richarde Elken', *M.G.H.* 5th series **2**, 1916-17, 26. 1464.

Elwes
'The p'ceedinge of the funerall of Geffrey Ellwes, esq., alderman of London', *M.G.H.* **2**, 1876, 2-3. 1616 list of mourners.
'Funeral certificate of Mrs Elizabeth Elwes, 1625', *M.G.H.* **2**, 1876, 4.

Fanshawe
'Fanshawe funeral certificates', *M.G.H.* **1**, 1868, 314-9. 1617th c.

Fisher
GATFIELD, GEORGE. 'Grant of arms to William Fisher, of the City of London, merchant, 1660', *Genealogist* N.S. **6**, 1890, 180.
'Grant of arms to William Fisher of London, merchant, 1660', *M.G.H.* 2nd series **2**, 1888, 228-9.

Franklin
'Funeral certificate: Richard Franklin of Willesdon, 1615', *M.G.H.* 2nd series **5**, 1894, 264.

Fuller
FULLER, JAMES FRANKLIN. 'Funeral certificate of Nicholas Fuller, 1619', *M.G.H.* N.S. **1**, 1874, 326-7. Includes pedigree, 16-17th c.

Gill
'Grants and confirmations of arms', *M.G.H.* 5th series **8**, 1932-4, 310-14. Includes grants to Gill of St.Pauls, 1614, and Gilpin of London, 1574.

Gilpin
See Gill

Glynn
'Funeral certificate: Sir John Glynn, 1666',
M.G.H. 2nd series 1, 1886, 43-4. Of
Lincoln's Inn Fields.

Gosfright
'Grants of arms', *M.G.H.* 5th series 5, 1923-5,
137-40. Includes grants to Gosfright, 1657,
and Hallydaye, 1605, both of London.

Greenhill
GRAZEBROOK, GEO. 'A heraldic and
physiological curiosity', *M.G.H.* 3rd series
5, 1904, 296-9. Greenhill family of
London; 17th c. arms.

Gull
'Augmentation of arms to Sir William
Withey Gull, Bart, 1872', *M.G.H.* N.S. 1,
1874, 453-4.

Hallydaye
See Gosfright

Hampson
'Grant of arms to Robert Hampson, alderman
of London, 1602', *M.G.H.* 2nd series 2,
1888, 218.

Harlyn
See Wylkynson

Hart
'Funeral certificate: Sir Eustace Hart, 1634',
M.G.H. 2nd series 1, 1886, 32. Of St.Benet,
Paul's Wharf.

Highlord
See Hillard

Hide
BANNERMAN, W. BRUCE. 'Funeral certificate
of Bernard Hide, esquire, 1631', *M.G.H.* 4th
series 3, 1910, 97.

Hillard
'Grant of crest to John and Zachary Hillard
alias Highlord, 1630', *M.G.H.* 3rd series 4,
1902, 37.

Hough
'Grant of arms to Ralph Hough, 1650',
M.G.H. 2nd series 1, 1886, 288.

Howley
'Grant of arms to William Howley, Bishop of
London 1813', *M.G.H.* N.S. 4, 1884, 6; 2nd
series 2, 1888, 330-31; 5, 1894, 81.

Humfrey
'Grant of arms and crest to William
Humfrey of London, 1562', *M.G.H.* 4th
series 1, 1906, 1-2.

Huxley
'Funeral certificate: George Huxley, 1627',
M.G.H. 2nd series 1, 1886, 188. Of
Edmonton.

Jason
'Grant of arms to Robert Jason of Enfield,
1588', *M.G.H.* 2nd series 3, 1890, 49-50.

Kenrick
'Kenrick bookplates', *M.G.H.* 5th series 9,
1935-7, 102. Of London and Surrey,
17-19th c.

Kimpton
'Grant of arms to William Kimpton, of
Monken Hadley, Co.Middlesex, esq.,
Alderman of London, by Robert Cooke,
Clarenceux, dated 3 April 1574', *M.G.H.* 1,
1868, 46-7.

Lear
'Grant of arms by Sir Edward Walker,
Garter, to Sir Peter Lear, Bart, 1660',
M.G.H. 3rd series 1, 1896, 233-4. Of Devon
and London.

Machell
'Funeral certificate of Thomas Machell of
Hackney, Co.Middlesex, gent', *M.G.H.* 4th
series 2, 1908, 16. 1581.

Makins
'Grant of arms to Charles Makins of Craven
Hill, Middlesex, 1872', *M.G.H.* N.S. 2, 1877,
34-5.

Malte
'Grant of arms to John Malte of London,
1544', *M.G.H.* 5th series 6, 1926-8, 1-2.

More

COLE, A. COLIN. 'Sir Thomas More's quartering ... and a new old grant', *Coat of arms* N.S., 1(93), 1975, 126-31.

Mosley

'Grant of crest and confirmation of arms to Nicholas Mosley, alderman of London, 1592', *M.G.H.* N.S. 3, 1880, 98.

Pearson

'Grant and confirmation of arms, by Garter, Clarenceaux, and Norroy, to Henry Robert Pearson, of London, gentleman sometime chief clerk in Her Majesty's Treasury, and to the other descendants of his late uncle, Thomas Pearson of Manchester, gentleman, A.D. 1865', *M.G.H.* 7, 1883, 231-2.

Percivall

'Funeral certificates', *M.G.H.* 2nd series 1, 1886, 149. For Thomas and Katherine Percivall, 1630 and 1633.

Penson

C[OKAYNE], G.E. 'Description of the arms surmounting the undated advertisement of Thomas Penson, armes painter', *M.G.H.* 3rd series 4, 1902, 109.

Perrot

'Confirmation of arms to George Perrot, 4 January, 3 Edward VI', *M.G.H.* 3rd series 3, 1900, 1-2. Of Pembrokeshire and London.

Prichard

'Funeral certificate of Sir William Prichard, Knt, 1705', *M.G.H.* N.S. 1, 1874, 351-2.

Raymond

'The E.M.'s warr't for a grant of arms to Sr Jonathan Raymond, Knt., alderm' of Lond', *M.G.H.* 2nd series 2, 1888, 59-60. 1687.

Raynie

'Funeral certificate', *M.G.H.* 1, 1868, 192. John Raynie of London, 1632.

Reyny

'Exemplification of arms and grant of crest by William Camden, Clarenceux to John Reyny of London, 1619', *M.G.H.* 1, 1868, 191.

Robarts

R[YLANDS], J.P. 'Grant of arms by Sir Isaac Heard, Garter, and Sir George Nayler, Clarenceux, to James Thomas Robarts of London, and to Charlotte his wife, daughter of Martin Allen Lloyd, deceased 12th June 1821', *M.G.H.* 4th series 5, 1913, 46-7.

Russell

'Arms and crest of John Russell of London, 1552', *M.G.H.* 3rd series 5, 1904, 121.

Sheldon

'Grant of arms to Gilbert Sheldon, D.D., Bishop of London, 1660', *M.G.H.* 2nd series 5, 1894, 1(f).

Starkey

'Grant of arms to Roger Starkey of London, 1543', *M.G.H.* 3rd series 3, 1900, 65.

Stone

'Grant of arms to Arthur Stone of the Inner Temple, 1729', *M.G.H.* 4th series 3, 1910, 230-31.

Sweetaple

'Grant of arms to Sir John Sweetaple, 1699', *M.G.H.* 2nd series 1, 1886, 133.

Talor

'Confirmation of arms and grant of crest to John Le Talor, 1572', *M.G.H.* 2nd series 4, 1892, 273-4.

Thornbery

LONDON, H. STANFORD. 'Thomas Thornbery, Windsor Herald, 17451757', *M.G.H.* 5th series 10, 1938, 79-80. Grant of arms.

Thornley

'Grant of arms to Stephen Thornley of London, 1655', *M.G.H.* 2nd series 2, 1888, 294.

Thoyts
'Grant of arms to William Thoyts of London, 1788', *M.G.H.* 2nd series **4**, 1892, 6.

Tryon
'Tryon arms', *M.G.H.* 5th series **10**, 1938, 107. 1610.

Turner
'Nathaniel Turner: alteration of arms, 1710', *M.G.H.* 2nd series **1**, 1886, 122.

Tymms
'Tymms: herald's certificate touching a coat of arms used at the funeral of Thomas Tymms of London, physician', *M.G.H.* 3rd series **5**, 1904, 129. 1687.

Tyssen
DANIEL-TYSSEN, J.R. 'Grant of arms to Francis Tyssen of London, 1687', *M.G.H.* N.S. **3**, 1880, 379-80. Includes pedigree, 17th c.

Vassall
'Armorial bookplate: Sir Spencer Lambert Hunter Vassall', *M.G.H.* 2nd series **4**, 1892, 120. 16-19th c.

Webbe
'Grant of arms to Henry Webbe, 1550', *M.G.H.* 3rd series **2**, 1898, 156.

Weld
'Grant of arms to John Weld of London, gent., 1559', *M.G.H.* 5th series **2**, 1916-17, 171-2.

West
'Grant of arms to John West of London, 1600', *M.G.H.* 3rd series **2**, 1898, 177.

Wise
WISE, H.C. 'Grant of arms to Henry Wise of Brompton Park, Middlesex, 1720', *M.G.H.* N.S. **1**, 1874, 201.

Wolstenholme
'Dame Anne Wolstenholme, 1661', *M.G.H.* 2nd series **2**, 1888, 118-20. Funeral certificate; also of Sir John Wolstenholme, 1670.

Woodmason
GREEN, EVERARD. 'Grant of arms and crest to John Woodmason of the City of London, 1790', *M.G.H.* 4th series **1**, 1906, 137.

Wylkynson
'Grant of arms to John Wylkynson *alias* Harlyn of the City of London, 3rd August 1519', *M.G.H.* 2nd series **2**, 1888, 201(f). Facsimile.

5. DIARIES, etc.

Diaries may be invaluable sources of family history, and frequently provide information concerning families quite unrelated to their authors. The pre-eminent English diarist, Samuel Pepys, was a Londoner, and no bibliography on the metropolis would be complete without a mention of his work. Not only does he give us many vignettes of life in his day; his diary also includes much information of direct genealogical volume. There are many editions; the best one is:
PEPYS, SAMUEL. *The diary of Samuel Pepys: a new and complete transcription,* ed. Robert Latham and William Matthews. 10 vols. Bell & Hyman, 1970-83. A companion volume is provided in v.10; this includes biographical notes on numerous persons mentioned.
A variety of other London diaries are also available, but they cannot all be listed here. See, however:

Baker
BAKER, JOHN. *The diary of John Baker, barrister of the Middle Temple, solicitor-general of the Leeward Islands, being extracts there from . . . a record of life, family history and society, 1751-1778 in England (mostly in Sussex and London) and the Leeward Islands, and of two travels abroad,* ed. Philip C. Yorke. Hutchinson & co., 1931. Includes pedigree, 17-18th c.

Beattie
BEATTIE, JAMES. *James Beattie's London diary, 1773,* ed. Ralph S. Walker. Aberdeen: Aberdeen University Press, 1946. Includes an appendix of biographical notes on many of those mentioned.

Brown
BROWN, FORD MADOX. *The diary,* ed. Virginia Surtees. New Haven: Yale University Press for the Paul Mellon Centre, 1981. Cover 1847-66.

Chaney
'Ebenezer Chaney's diary, 1890-1891', *U.R.* **55**, 1991, 7-12; **56**, 1991, 6-7; **57**, 1992, 13-14. Includes pedigree, 19th c.

Garnett
GARNETT, OLIVE. *Tea and anarchy: the Bloomsbury diary of Olive Garnett, 1890-1893,* ed. Barry C. Johnson. Bartlett Press, 1989. Includes a 'who's who' of people mentioned.
GARNETT, OLIVE. *Olive & Stepniak: the Bloomsbury diary of Olive Garnett, 1893-1895,* ed. Barry C. Johnson. Birmingham: Bartletts Press, 1993. Includes a 'who's who' of persons mentioned.

Lever
WALLIS, ALFRED. 'The diary of a London citizen in the seventeenth century', *Reliquary* N.S. **3**, 1889, 90-98; **4**, 1890, 135-41; **5**, 1891, 13-20. Includes much genealogical information on the Lever family.

Machyn
NICHOLS, JOHN GOUGH, ed. *The diary of Henry Machyn, citizen and merchant-taylor of London, from A.D.1550 to A.D.1563.* Camden Society old series **42**. 1848. Includes notes on many funerals.

Nicolson
JONES, CLIVE, & HOLMES, GEOFFREY, eds. *The London diaries of William Nicolson, Bishop of Carlisle, 1702-1718.* Oxford: Clarendon Press, 1983. Appendix A provides biographical notes on many persons mentioned.

Raikes
RAIKES, THOMAS. *A portion of a journal kept from 1831 to 1847, comprising reminiscences of social and political life in London and Paris during that period.* New ed. 2 vols. Longmans, 1858. A 'society' diary.

Sambourne
NICHOLSON, SHIRLEY. *A Victorian household.* Barrie & Jenkins, 1988. Based on the diaries of Marion Sambourne; includes Sambourne pedigree, 19-20th c.

6. FAMILY HISTORIES, etc.

A considerable amount of research on Metropolitan family history has been published. This list includes published books and journal articles; it does not, however, include the numerous notes and queries published in journals such as *N.M.*, except where substantial information is provided. Studies which remain unpublished are not listed; nor are newspaper articles.

Many pedigrees of particular families are listed here; however, those which are included in the collections of pedigrees cited in section 4, or in section 7 of Stuart Raymond's *English genealogy: a bibliography*, have not been separately listed.

Abbott
ABBOT, JASPER A.R. 'Robert Abbott, city money scrivener, and his account book, 1646-1652', *Gl.M.* 1(7), 1952-60, 31-9. General description of an account book, including some names, with genealogical notes on Abbott.

Agace
WAGNER, HENRY. 'Family of Agace', *Pr.Hug.Soc.L.* 11, 1915-17, 152-4. Folded pedigree, 18th c.

Agnew
AGNEW, GEOFFREY. *Agnew's, 1817-1967.* Bradbury Agnew Press, 1967. Picture dealers; includes pedigree of Agnew, 18-20th c., also lists of staff.

Allen
ALLEN, JAMES A. *The Allen chronicle: a family in war and peace.* Braunton: Merlin Books, 1988. Of Herefordshire and London.

ALLEN, WILLIAM E.D. *David Allens: the history of a family firm 1857-1957.* John Murray, 1957.

Amyand
WAGNER, HENRY. 'Huguenot refugee family of Amyand', *M.G.H.* N.S. 4, 1884, 180-81. 18-19th c.

Anderson
MUIR, CHARLES AUGUSTUS. *Andersons of Islington: the history of C.F. Anderson and Son Ltd., 1863-1963.* Newman Neave, 1963. Timber merchants; history of a family business.

André
WAGNER, HENRY. 'Pedigree of André', *Pr.Hug.Soc.L.* 10, 191214, 485-90. Folded pedigrees, 16-19th c.

Andrews
POYNTON, F.J. 'Notes relating to the family of Andrews', *M.G.H.* N.S. 3, 1880, 160-61 & 169-71. 17-18th c., from a family prayer book.

Anthony
ANTHONY, CHARLES L. *Genealogy of the Anthony family from 1495 to 1904, from William Anthony, Cologne, Germany, to London, England; John Anthony, a descendant, from England to America. With photographs and biographical sketches of the lives of prominent men and women.* Sterling, Ill: the author, 1904.

Archer
See Deacon

Ardesoif
WAGNER, HENRY. 'A fragmentary pedigree of Ardesoif: Thomas Ardesoif, and his immediate descendants', *M.G.H.* 4th series 3, 1910, 215-6. Pedigree, 18-19th c.

MERCER, R.V.F. *John Arnold and Son, chronometer makers, 1762-1843.* Antiquarian Horological Society, 1972. Of Bodmin and St.Winnow, Cornwall, and London; includes wills.

Ashby
G., H. 'Genealogical notices of the family of Ashby of Harefield in the County of Middlesex', *C.T.G.* 5, 1838, 125-41. Includes pedigree, 17-19th c.

Aspinall
GROUNDS, TOM. 'A Tottenham to Waterloo return', *N.M.* 9, 1987, 10-13. Aspinall family, 19th c.

Atkin

GRUGEON, BRIAN. 'Norton Lees & the Atkin family: a postscript to the Muswell Hill outrage', *Hornsey Historical Society bulletin* **32**, 1991, 34-8. Includes pedigree of Atkin, 19-20th c.

Atlee

HARPER-SMITH, T., & A. *The Atlees of Acton, Ealing, Hammersmith, Hillingdon, and the U.S.A.* Acton past & present **8**. Acton History Group, 1986. 16-19th c.

Auber

WAGNER, HENRY. 'Pedigree of Auber', *M.G.H.* 4th series **1**, 1906, 93-5. 18-19th c.

Audley

READ, ALEYN LYELL. *Audley pedigrees.* Percy Lund Humphries & Co., 1926. Includes 'Audley of Buckingham and Fulham', 'Audley of Holborn and of Beales, Co. Suffolk', 'Audley of London and Rotherhithe', and 'Audley of St. Dunstan in the East and of Stepney'; also of many other counties.

Aufrère

TURNER, WINIFRED, ed. *The Aufrère papers: calendar and selections.* Publications of the Huguenot Society of London **40**. 1940. Papers of the Aufrère family, 17-18th c. Includes pedigree.

Augard

COLLINS, LYN, & MARRUS, JOHN. *Two centuries of the Augard family, 1789-1989: Augard family history.* Abingdon: Abbey Press, 1991. Of London and New Zealand.

Ayrton

WILLETTS, PAMELA. 'The Ayrton papers: music in London, 1786-1858', *British Library journal* **6**, 1980, 7-23. Discussion of Ayrton family papers.

Bagnall

See Skilbeck

Baily

See Saunders

Baker

ROBBINS, MICHAEL. 'The Baker of Baker Street', *London journal* **12**, 1986, 56-7. Answers the question, which member of the Baker family was Baker Street named after? 18-19th c.

SHEPPARD, FRANCES. *Robert Baker of Piccadilly Hall and his heirs.* Publication **127**. London Topographical Society, 1982. Includes pedigrees of the Bakers of Staplegrove, Somerset, and Piccadilly, 16-17th c.

Barclay

BARCLAY, CHARLES W., *et al. History of the Barclay family, with full pedigree from 1066 to [1933].* 3 vols. St.Catherine Press, 1923-4. Of Gloucestershire, Scotland, London, Walthamstow, Essex, and Dorking, Surrey.

Bard

S[TEINMAN], G.S. 'Pedigree of Bard of Lincolnshire, Middlesex and Bucks., and Viscount Bellamonte of the Kingdom of Ireland', *C.T.G.* **4**, 1837, 59-61. 16-18th c.

Barefoot

BAREFOOT, MICHAEL. *Why they came to London.* Bovey Tracey: the author, 1992? Barefoot, Moss, James, McIntosh, Pepperell families in early 19th c. London.

Barham

MURGATROYD, A.H. 'Some notes on the Barhams and Barham Park', *W.H.S.J.* **4**(1), 1975, 15-19.

Baril

See Berchere

Baring

ORBELL, JOHN. *Baring Brothers and Co. Ltd. a history to 1939.* Baring Brothers & Co., 1985. Includes folded pedigree, 18-20th c.

ZIEGLER, PHILIP SANDEMAN. *The sixth great power: Barings, 1762-1929.* Collins, 1988. Includes pedigrees of Baring, 17-20th c.

Barker
KELLEY, LILLIAN W. 'New light on the life and family of the Rev. John Barker of Hackney and of Salters Hall', *Journal of the Presbyterian Historical Society of England* **4**, 1928-31, 164-73. 18th c., also concerns Raymond family.

Barltrop
BARLTROP, ROBERT. *The Bar tree: a family history: Barltrop, Bartrip, Bartrop, Bartrick, Barthropp, Bartrup.* R. Barltrop, 1979. 14-20th c., includes pedigrees.

Barnes
BARNES, ARTHUR HARMAN. *History of a family: Barnes.* Aughton: A.H. Barnes, 1971. Supplement, 1971. 18-20th c.
SAGE, EDWARD J. 'Barnes pedigree: additions to the visitation of London, A.D. 1568, recently published by the Harleian Society', *M.G.H.* N.S. **1**, 1874, 78-9.

Barraud
BARRAUD, E.M. *Barraud: the story of a family.* Research Publishing, 1967. 18-20th c. Includes pedigrees.
JAGGER, CEDRIC SARGEANT. *Paul Philip Barraud: a study of a fine chronometer maker and of his relatives, associates and successors, in the family business, 1750-1929.* Antiquarian Horological Society, 1968. Supplement, 1979. Includes wills.

Barritt
BARRITT, MARY. *The Barritts of Wapping High Street.* OO Publications, 1979. 20th c.

Barrow
ROUND, J. HORACE. 'An early citizen squire', *Ancestor* **2**, July 1902, 58-62. Barrow family; includes pedigree, 11-13th c.

Barry
ADKINS, KATHLEEN. *The Barry/Rosell family saga: forbears and descendants of Walter Edward Barry (1757-1805) and his links with Samuel Rowsell (1777-1858) and his family.* Canterbury: Family History Productions, 1978. 18-19th c.

Bartrip, Bartrop, etc.
See Barltrop

Baster
NOBLE, JEAN C. 'A photographic mystery story', *Family tree magazine* **10**(3), 1994, 21-3. Baster family, 18-19thc., of London, Essex and Norfolk.

Batt
'The Copse & the Batt family', *W.D.D.H.* **24**, 1966, 3-6. At West Drayton; 18-20th c.

Bayne
See Heaton

Bayning
GILLESPIE, HUGH G. 'The rediscovery of an Elizabethan merchant adventurer', *Genealogists' magazine* **9**, 1940-46, 429-33. Paul Bayning, 1539-1616.

Beauclerk
ADAMSON, DONALD, & DEWAR, PETER BEAUCLERK. *The house of Nell Gwyn: the fortunes of the Beauclerk family, 1670-1974.* William Kimber, 1974. Also of Lincolnshire and Nottinghamshire. Dukes of St.Albans.

Beaufoy
KERR, BARBARA. *The dispossessed: an aspect of Victorian social history.* John Baker, 1974. Beaufoy and Thornhill families of Stanmore and Bushey. Includes pedigrees, 18-20th c.

Beckman
HERRIDGE, KEVIN. 'The family Beckman(n)', *C.A.* **41**, 1988-9, 15-18. 19-20th c.

Bedell
BEDELLS, J.H.B. 'The alderman of London', *Family history* **14**(114) 1987, 226-30. Mathew Bedell and his ancestry.

Bellamy
BUSHELL, W. DONE. *The Bellamies of Uxendon.* Harrow Octocentenary Tracts **14**. Cambridge: Bowes and Bowes, 1914. Includes pedigree, 15-16th c.

BUSHELL, W. DONE. 'The Bellamies of Uxendon', *T.L.M.A.S.* N.S. **3**, 1917, 71-104. Includes pedigree, 15-16th c.

Benham
BOWERS, FAITH. 'The Benhams of Bloomsbury', *Baptist quarterly* N.S., **19**(2), 1981, 64-76. 19th c.

Benne
'Benne pedigree', *M.G.H.* 2nd series **1**, 1886, 140-43 & 157. Of London and Surrey, 16-17th c. Includes monumental inscriptions, will of Sir Anthony Benne, 1618, *etc.*

Bennett
DANIEL-TYSSEN, J.R. 'Bennett of Hackney: extracts from the registers of St.Johns Church, Hackney, relating to the Bennett family', *M.G.H.* **1**, 1868, 297-8.
HARRISON, A.D. 'Citizens and pewterers of London', *Essex review* **72**(168), 1933, 169-75. Bennett family, 17th c.
SHERWOOD, P.T., & WHITE, B.T. 'The Bennet's of Dawley', *J.H.H.L.H.S.* **25**, 1982, 6-9 & **27**, 1983, 13-14. 17-19th c.

Benolt
LAMBARDE, FRANK. 'Clarenceux Benolt', *M.G.H.* 5th series **8**, 1932-4, 257-9. Notes on a heraldic family, 16th c., with pedigree.

Benson
MACLEOD, JUDITH. *The Benson letter book, 1837-1916: a Benson family history.* Turramurra, N.S.W.: the author, 1990? Of London, Cork and Australia. *See also* Strachey

Bentley
'A pedigree of the family of Bentley', *M.G.H.* N.S. **3**, 1880, 94(f). Of Shropshire and London, 17-18th c.

Berchere
WAGNER, HENRY. 'Pedigree of the Huguenot refugee families of Berchere and Baril', *Genealogist* N.S. **23**, 1907, 248-51. 17-18th c.

Berkeley
FALK, BERNARD. *The Berkeleys of Berkeley Square & some of their kinsfolk.* Hutchinson & Co., 1944. 17-20th c.

Berry
See Ferguson

Beuzeville
BEUZEVILLE, W.A. 'Notes on the family of Beuzeville', *Pr.Hug.Soc.L.* **12**, 1917-23, 417-21. 18-19th c.

Bevan
GAMBLE, AUDREY NONA. *History of the Bevan family.* Headley, 1924. Includes pedigree, 17-19th c.

Bicknell
See Browne

Billingsley
'Billingsley pedigree', *M.G.H.* **1**, 1868, 125-6. 16-17th c.

Biscoe
JONES, A.G.E. 'John Biscoe: tracing a master mariner', *Local historian* **8**(5), 1969, 160-66. Illustrates how to trace an early 19th c. seaman.

Bishop
WAINWRIGHT, DAVID. *Stone's ginger wine: fortunes of a family firm, 1740-1990.* Quiller Press, 1990. Bishop family business; includes pedigree, 18-20th c.

Blades
See De La Pryme

Blunt
BLUNT, REGINALD. *Memoirs of Gerald Blunt of Chelsea, his family and forbears.* Truslove & Hanson, 1911. Includes folded pedigree of Blunt of Sussex, medieval-20th c.

Blutte
MINET, WILLIAM. 'The family of Blutte', *Pr.Hug.Soc.L.* **11**, 1915-17, 381-6. 18-19th c.

Boddington
BODDINGTON, REGINALD STEWART. 'Boddington pedigree', *M.G.H.* N.S. **2**, 1877, 545-8. 16-18th c.
BODDINGTON, REGINALD STEWART. 'Bodington – Boddington – Sheppard – Petty', *M.G.H.* 2nd series **5**, 1894, 334-5, 343-5 & 358-60. 16-18th c.

'Memoranda relating to the families allied to that of Boddington', *M.G.H.* N.S. 3, 1880, 254-8. Pedigrees of Halford of London, 17-18th c., extracts from Hackney parish registers concerning Dolins family, 18th c., *etc.,* pedigree of Gray of Enfield, 17th c.

Bolt
WHITE, E.A. 'Bolt family: extracts from the fly-leaves of a bible ...', *M.G.H.* N.S. 2, 1877, 397-8. 18-19th c.

Bolton
BOLTON, CHARLES KNOWLES. 'The Boltons of Warwick, London and Madeira', *M.G.H.* 5th series 8, 1932-4, 287-92. 16-17th c.

Boothby
See Willan

Boulier
WAGNER, HENRY. 'Huguenot refugee families of Boulier de Beauregard and Gilbert and their immediate descendants', *Pr.Hug.Soc.L.* 11, 1915-17, 426-33. Folded pedigree, 18th c.

Bowater
WOODS, ALBERT WILLIAM. 'The pedigree of Sir Edward Bowater', *M.G.H.* N.S. 2, 1877, 177-82. Of Coventry, Warwickshire, and London, *etc.,* 16-19th c.

Bradbrooke
BRADBROOKE, WILLIAM. *The Bradbrooke family register.* Privately printed, 1935. Of Norfolk, Buckinghamshire, Bethnal Green, Middlesex and Inkberrow, Worcestershire, *etc.*

Brassey
BODDINGTON, REGINALD STEWART. 'Brassey pedigree', *M.G.H.* N.S. 2, 1877, 577-80. Of London and Hertfordshire; 18-19th c.

Briklesworth
STOCKEN, JOHN J. 'The Briklesworths of London and Northampton', in PHILLIMORE, W.P.W., ed. *The London & Middlesex notebook.* Elliot Stock, 1892, 209-11. 14th c.

Bromfield
BURNBY, J.G.L. *Plague, pills & surgery: the story of the Bromfields.* Occasional paper N.S. 31. E.H.H.S., 1975. Includes Bromfield pedigree, 18-19th c.

Bromley
See Brown

Brooke
See Wittewronge

Brooker
BROOKER, DEREK HARRY NAYLOR. 'The Brookers in Sunbury on Thames', *J.S.S.L.H.S.* 18, 1986, 16-19. 19-20th c.

Brown
MORRIS, D.B. 'Mile End old town and the East India Company', *East London Record* 9, 1986, 20-27. Ships masters; includes notes on the Brown, Fitzhugh, Heath, Lane, Leake, Slater, Sullivan and Winter families, 18th c.

PADEN, W.D. 'The ancestry and families of Ford Madox Brown', *Bulletin of the John Ryland Library* 50, 1967-8, 124-35. 19th c., includes notes on Madox, Bromley and Hill families.

Browne
BICKNELL, A. SIDNEY. *Five generations: Bicknell of Taunton; Bicknell of Bridgwater; Bicknell of Farnham; Browne (Le Brune) of France and Spitalfields; Wilde of High Wycombe.* George Sherwood, 1912. Medieval-19th c. Includes pedigrees.

MARSHALL, CHARLES W. *The Browne family of Bristol, London, etc., from the mid-seventeenth century.* Exeter: the author, 1979.

M[ORGAN], G[EORGE] B[LACKER]. *Genealogical memoirs of the Browne family of Coverswell and Shredicote, Co.Stafford; Bentley Hall, Co.Derby; Greenford, Co.Middlesex; Withington and Caughley, Co.Salop; also of the Peploe family of Garnstone, Co.Hereford.* Mitchell & Hughes, 1888. Pedigrees, 17-19th c.
See also Warner

Brydges
BAKER, C.H. COLLINS. 'Lady Chandos'
register', *Genealogists' magazine* **10**, 1947-
50, 255-64, 299-309 & 339-52. Births,
marriages and deaths of the Brydges
family, 1642-1768.

Buckby
See Osborne

Bulstrode
MORRIS, GILLIAN M. *The history of
Hounslow manor and the Bulstrode
family.* Isleworth: Hounslow and District
History Society, 1980. 17-19th c.

Burney
HILL, CONSTANCE. *The house in St.Martins
Street: being chronicles of the Burney
family.* John Lane, 1907. 18th c.

Burnham
See Deacon

Burns
RYDEN, RAYMOND. 'The family of James
Burns, the convert Catholic publsher',
Catholic ancestor **5**(2), 1994, 59-63.
19th c.

Bushell
WHITEBROOK, J.C. 'Bushell of Frodsham',
*Congregational History Society
transactions* **6**, 1913-15, 379-88. Also of
Bishopsgate and Barbados; includes folded
pedigree, 17th c.

Butler
See Heaton

Cadogan
PEARMAN, ROBERT. *The Cadogan estate: the
history of a landed family.* Haggerston
Press, 1986.

Candeler
CHANDLER, JOHN. 'The Candelers of London',
Home counties magazine **6**, 1904, 232-4.
16-17th c. family.

Capper
See Wittewronge

Carnall
RICHARDS, PHILIP. 'Seventeenth century
Cockney cowkeepers and brickmakers',
C.A. **17**, 1982-3, 2-8; **18**, 1983, 2-6; **19**, 1983,
2-7. Carnall family; includes pedigree; also
includes pedigrees of Gisby and Pitt.

Carpue
ADOLPH, ANTHONY R.J.S. 'The Carpue family
of London', *Catholic ancestor* **4**(1), 1992,
7-13. Includes pedigree, 18-19th c.

Carvick
DENDY, R.S. 'Carvick: entries on fly-leaves of
the Carvick family bible', *M.G.H.* 3rd
series **3**, 1900, 197. 19th c.

Cawston
BEHRENS, LILIAN BOYS. *Echoes of the good
and fallen angels, de Cawston, Norfolk.*
Battle: Olivers Print Works, 1956. Includes
much on the Cawston family in London.

Cely
HANHAM, ALISON. *The Celys and their
world: an English merchant family of the
fifteenth century.* Cambridge: Cambridge
University Press, 1985. Includes pedigree,
15-16th c.
HANHAM, ALISON. *The Cely letters, 1472-
1488.* Early English Text Society **273**.
Oxford University Press, 1975. Letters of a
London merchant family, with notes on
the family.

Chamberlain
CHAMBERLAIN, JOAN. 'By any other name',
W.M. **3**(4), 1983, 91-3. Chamberlain family
of London and Richmond, Surrey; includes
pedigree, 18-20th c.

Chambers
MARCHAM, FRANK. 'The Chambers family: a
correction', *T.L.M.A.S.* N.S. **7**, 1937, 619-20.
18th c., brief note.

Chandos
See Brydges

Chapman
MURRAY, KEITH W. 'Chapman of
Hertfordshire and London', *Genealogist*
N.S. **34**, 1918, 1-5. 16-17th c.

WATERS, R.E. CHESTER. 'Chapman', *M.G.H.*
N.S. **1,** 1874, 5-6. Includes pedigree
of Chapman of St.Lawrence Jewry,
17-18th c.
'Extracts from the register of St.Lawrence
Jewry and St.Peter le Poor, relating to
the Chapman family', *M.G.H.* N.S. **1,**
1874, 8.

Charrington
STRONG, L.A.G. *A brewer's progress, 1757-
1957: a survey of Charrington's brewery
on the occasion of its bicentenary.*
Privately printed, 1957. Includes pedigree
of Charrington, 17-20th c.

Chase
See Waldo

Chasemore
CHASEMORE, FRANK. 'The merchant of
Fulham', *W.M.* **14**(1), 1996, 19-27. Includes
pedigree of Chasemore, 19th c.

Chasserau
WAGNER, HENRY. 'Huguenot pedigree of
Chasserau', *M.G.H.* N.S. **4,** 1884, 149-51. 18-
19th c.

Chater
See Grosvenor

Chaucer
CROW, MARTIN M, & OLSON, CLAIR C.
Chaucer life records. Oxford: Clarendon
Press, 1966. 14th c., includes notes on his
family, and many extracts from original
sources.

Cheever
See Gore

Chester
'Extracts from parish registers relating to Sir
Francis Chester, Bart', *M.G.H.* N.S. **1,**
1874, 29. Hackney; 18th c.

Child
LANG, M.E. 'The Childs of Osterley House &
the Jersey inheritance', *Honeslaw
chronicle* **8**(1), 1985, 6-10.

Churchill
MUIR, AUGUSTUS. *Churchill and Sim, 1813-
1963: a short history.* Newman Neame,
1963. Family firm of timber brokers;
includes pedigree shewing relationship of
Churchill, Clark and Sim, 19-20th c.

Clark(e)
GREEN, EVERARD. 'Pedigree of the family of
Clarke of Swakeleys in the County of
Middlesex', *M.G.H.* 4th series **1,** 1906,
16-15. 17-20th c.
See also Churchill

Clarkson
JENKIN, ROGER. *The wig-making Clarksons:
in search of their lives and times.*
Ilfracombe: Arthur H. Stockwell, 1982.
19th c.

Clifford
See Turner

Clowes
CLOWES, W.B. *Family business, 1803-1953.*
William Clowes and Sons, [1953]. Includes
pedigree of Clowes, 17-20th c.

Clutterbuck
HEWLETT, GEOFFREY. 'The Clutterbuck
family', *W.H.S.J.* **3**(10), 1975, 204-5 & 208.
18-20th c.

Coates
See Russell

Cockayne
COKAYNE, G.E. 'Cockayne pedigree', *M.G.H.*
3rd series **3,** 1900, 221-30. Of Derbyshire,
London, *etc.,* 13-17th c.

Cocks
SOMERS COCKS, J.V. *A history of the Cocks
family, Pt.II: Bishops Cleeve, London,
Harkstead, Crowle.* Teignmouth:
Brunswick Press, 1966. Bishops Cleeve,
Gloucestershire; Harkstead, Suffolk;
Crowle, Worcestershire. Includes
pedigrees, 17-18th c., with wills, *etc.*

Colchin
GOULSTONE, JOHN. 'Long Robin and the
cricketing Colchins', *Genealogists'
magazine* **24**(9), 1994, 389-93. Colchin
family 18th c.

Cole

LOFTUS, E.A. *A history of the descendants of Maximilian Cole of Oxford, who flourished in the 17th century.* Adlard & Son, 1938. Of Oxfordshire and London; includes folded pedigree in pocket.

MERCER, G.E. *The Cole papers: the Coles of Heatham House, Twickenham: the brewery and the Cole Park and Amyand Park estates, 1575-1901.* B.T.L.H.S. paper **56**, 1985. Includes pedigree.

See also Gore

Colet

COLLET, CLARA E. 'The family of Dean Colet: summary of facts obtained from the records of the Mercer's Company', *Genealogists' magazine* **7**, 1935-7, 242-3. 15th c.

Collet

CHADD, MARGARET. *The Collet saga.* Norwich: Elvery Dowers, 1988. Gloucestershire, Suffolk and London; includes pedigrees, 16-20th c.

LAURIE, PETER R. *Our Collett ancestors: a family memoir.* Brentwood: Wilson and Whitworth, 1898. Includes folded pedigree, 15-19th c.

Collier

BODDINGTON, REGINALD STEWART. 'Pedigree of the family of Collier', *M.G.H.* N.S. **3**, 1880, 125-9. 18-19th c.

Comarque

WAGNER, HENRY. 'Pedigree of the Huguenot family of Comarque', *M.G.H.* 4th series **1**, 1906, 315. Of London and Surrey; 18th c.

Combrune

WAGNER, HENRY. 'The Huguenot refugee family of Combrune', *Genealogist* N.S. **24**, 1908, 194-5. 18th c.

WAGNER, HENRY. 'Huguenot refugee family (extinct) of Combrune', *M.G.H.* 4th series **1**, 1906, 43-4. Pedigree, 18th c.

Conant

See Horton

Congreve

HAYNES, JEAN. 'My Congreve family', *N.M.* **7**(3), 1985, 72-5. Mainly 18-19th c.

Cooke

'Pedigree of Cooke', *M.G.H.* 2nd series **4**, 1892, 152. Of Harefield, 18-19th c.

Cooper

NEWDIGATE, C.A. 'Entries in a Douay New Testament, 1761-1770', *L.R.* **2**, 1972, 41-2. Cooper family entries.

See also Dickens

Cope

See Rea

Copland

BROCK, RICHARD E. *The Copland-Crawfords of Wembley.* Ware: the author, 1989. 19th c.

BROCK, RICHARD E. 'The Copland-Crawfords of Wembley', *W.H.S.J.* **6**(10), 1992, 206-14; **7**(1), 1992, 230-39. 19th c. To be continued.

Cornwallis

MORIARTY, G.ANDREWS 'The early generations of Cornwallis of Brome', *N.E.H.G.R.* **110** 1956, 122-7. 14-16th c. Brome, Suffolk; originally of London.

Corsellis

CULLUM, G. MILNER GIBSON. 'The Corsellis family', *M.G.H.* 5th series **1**, 1916, 57-63 & 105-13. See also 158-9. London and Essex; 17-19th c. Includes wills, notes from membership list of the Dutch Reformed Church, London, extracts from parish registers and monumental inscriptions.

CULLUM, G. MILNER GIBSON. *Pedigree of the family of Corsellis, with abstracts from wills, parish registers, etc.* Mitchell & Hughes, 1914. Reprinted from *M.G.H.* Of London and Essex; 16-19th c., includes wills, parish register extracts, *etc.*

CULLUM, G. MILNER GIBSON. 'Pedigree of the family of Corsellis', *M.G.H.* 5th series **1**, 1916, 19-27. See also 5th series **2**, 1916-17, 154. London, Wivenhoe, Essex, *etc.* 16-19th c.

Coster

EDWARDS, GERALD KENNETH SAVERY HAMILTON. *Pedigree of the family of Coster of London, Witheridge, Devon and of New Zealand.* [Plymouth?]: [the author?], 1944.

Cotterell
SHERWOOD, PHILLIP. 'The Cott(e)rell family in Harlington', *W.M.* **3**(4), 1983, 94-5. 17-19th c.

Courtauld
COURTALD, S.L. *The Huguenot family of Courtauld.* 3 vols. Privately printed, 1957. Of France, London, Essex and the United States; includes folded pedigrees, 16-19th c., in separate wallet.

Courteen
MOENS, W.J.C. 'Pedigree of Courteen', *M.G.H.* 2nd series **2**, 1888, 158-60. London, *etc.*; 15-17th c.

Coutts
RICHARDSON, RALPH. *Coutts and Co., bankers, Edinburgh and London, being the memoirs of a family distinguished for its public services in England and Scotland.* Elliot Stock, 1902.

Coward
HIGGS, JOYCE. 'Have you a Coward in your family?', *H.F.H.S.M.* **19**, 1992, 9-10. 19th c. Coward family.

Cox
JONES, KENNETH R. 'A hundred years at Hillingdon House: a history of the Cox family', *U.R.* **8**, 1967, 14-18 & 7. 19-20th c.
JONES, KENNETH RONALD. *The Cox's of Craig's Court and Hillingdon.* Watford: K.R. Jones, 1969. Includes pedigree, 18-20th c.

Cranmer
WATERS, ROBERT EDMOND CHESTER. *Genealogical memoirs of the kindred families of Thomas Cranmer, Archbishop of Canterbury, and Thomas Wood, Bishop of Lichfield, illustrated with twelve short pedigrees, engravings of all Archbishop Cranmer's official seals, and shields of arms.* Robson and Sons, 1877. Cranmer of Mitcham, Surrey, Aslacton, Norfolk, Astwoodbury, Buckinghamshire and Loudham, Suffolk. Wood of Hackney, Kensington and Suffolk. Includes pedigrees, 15-16th c.

Crawford
See Copland

Crawley
See Gibbs

Creamor
See Haydock

Creffield
ROUND, J.H. 'The Creffield family', *Genealogist* N.S. **3**, 1898, 80-83. Of London and Surrey; includes 18th c. pedigree.

Cressett
SYKES, JOHN. 'Cressett', *M.G.H.* N.S. **1**, 1874, 31. Pedigree, 17th c.

Creuzé
WAGNER, HENRY. 'A tentative pedigree of the (now extinct) Huguenot refugee family of Creuzé', *Genealogist* N.S. **27**, 1911, 114-5. 18th c.
See also Ogier

Crispe
CRISP, FREDERICK ARTHUR. *Collections relating to the family of Crispe.* 4 vols. Privately published, 1897. vol. 1. Abstracts of wills and administration in the Prerogative Court of Canterbury, 1516-1760. Vol.2. Grants of arms, funeral certificates and pedigrees from the records of the College of Arms. v.3. Abstracts of wills and administration in the courts of the Archdeacon of Suffolk, 1454-1800. v.4. Miscellanea. Of London, Suffolk and many other counties.

Cruden
WILD, M. 'Marriage and madness', *W.M.* **5**(3), 1985, 69-73; **5**(4), 1985, 101-5. Cruden family of West Middlesex and South Buckinghamshire, 18th c.

Cruso
'Cruso pedigree', *M.G.H.* **1**, 1868, 229. 17th c.

Cufley
CUFLEY, DAVID. 'Cufley: a one name study', *N.M.* **8**(4), 1986, 89-92.

Cullum
CULLUM, G. MILNER GIBSON. 'Cullum',
M.G.H. 2nd series 1, 1886, 181-4, 197-8,
286-7, 302-8, 348-51 & 373-6; 2, 1888, 2-6,
73-4, 170-2, 193-4, 230-31, 351-2 & 355-6; 3,
1890, 139-40, 315-6 & 328; 4, 1892, 25-7,
175-6, 221-3, 238-40, 320 & 369-70; 5,
1894, 5-6, 31-2, 39-40, 55-6, 67-8, 92-4, 97-
8, 117-9, 1412, 154-7, 163-5, 182-5, 193-7,
220-23, 290-93, 310-13, 325-7, 340-42,
353-4 & 369-71. Of Suffolk and London;
pedigrees, extracts from parish
registers, monumental inscriptions, wills,
etc., etc.

Curtis
'William Curtis, F.L.S., eminent botanist',
M.G.H. 5th series 4, 1920-22, 150-54.
18th c.

Curtoys
'Memoranda of William Curtoys, 1670-
1752', *M.G.H.* 3rd series 5, 1904, 34-7 &
69-73.

Dalgety
DAUNTON, M.J. 'Firm and family in the City
of London in the nineteenth century: the
case of F.G. Dalgety', *Historical research*
62(148), 1989, 154-77.

Daunse
CARPINELLI, FRANK. 'Thomas More and the
Daunse family', *Albion* 10(supplement),
1978, 1-10. 16th c.

Davall
BERTHON, RAYMOND TINNE. 'The family of
Peter Davall, F.R.S., Master in Chancery',
Genealogist N.S. 31, 1915, 223-38. Of
London and Essex; 17-18th c. Includes
wills.

Davies
GREEN, EVERARD. 'The true descent of Mary
Davis, who brought the Grosvenors their
London property', *Middlesex &
Hertfordshire notes & queries* 2, 1896, 189.
Pedigree of Davies, 16-17th c.

Dayrolles
See Teissoniere

De Burgh
COX, A.H. 'The De Burgh family of West
Drayton', *W.D.D.H.* 32, 1969, 5-7. 19th c.

De Cerjat
See D'Hervart

De La Chaumette
WAGNER, HENRY. 'Pedigree of the family of
De La Chaumette', *M.G.H.* 4th series 2,
1908, 176-7. 19th c.

De La Pryme
F., B.A. 'De La Pryme and Blades', *M.G.H.*
N.S. 3, 1880, 227. From family bible, 17-
18th c.

De Mainbray
WAGNER, HENRY. 'Pedigree of De Mainbray',
Genealogist N.S. 27, 1911, 22-3. 18th c.

De Salis
WHITE, B.T. 'The De Salis family at
Harlington', *J.H.H.L.H.S.* 37, 1988, 3-4.
18th c.

De St.Leu
WAGNER, HENRY. 'Extinct Huguenot refugee
family of De St.Leu', *M.G.H.* 4th series 1,
1906, 155. 18th c.

Deacon
DEACON, CATHARINE A. *Records of the
family of Deacon of Kettering and
London, with notices of allied families.*
Mitchell & Hughes, 1899. Includes folded
pedigrees, 17-19th c. The allied families
are Archer, Grover, Osborn and Burnham.
DEACON, EDWARD. *The descent of the family
of Deacon of Elstowe and London, with
some genealogical, biographical and
topographical notes, and sketches of allied
families, including Reynes of Clifton and
Meres of Kirton.* Bridgeport, Connecticut:
privately published, 1898. Includes
pedigrees, medieval-19th c. Elstowe,
Bedfordshire; Clifton Reynes,
Buckinghamshire; Kirton, Lincolnshire.

Debonnaire
WAGNER, HENRY. 'Pedigree of the Huguenot
refugee family of Debonnaire', *M.G.H.*
N.S. 3, 1880, 245-8. 17-19th c.

Delaforce
DELAFORCE, PATRICK. *Family history research, vol.1: the French connection.* Regency Press, 1983. 16-20th c.

Delamare
WAGNER, HENRY. 'Pedigree of the Huguenot refugee family of Delamare', *M.G.H.* 4th series **2**, 1908, 318-9. 18-19th c.

Denny
DENNY, H.L.L. 'Pedigrees of some East Anglian Dennys', *Genealogist* N.S., **38**, 1922, 15-28. Traces descent from a London family, 15-17th c.

Descarrierres
BRADBROOKE, WILLIAM. 'The French Huguenot refugee family of Descarrierres', *M.G.H.* 3rd series **4**, 1902, 77-80. See also 151 & 227. Includes pedigree, 17-19th c., wills, and extracts from Bethnal Green parish registers, 18-19th c.

D'Hervart
WAGNER, HENRY. 'Pedigree of D'Hervart, De Cerjat, and Winn', *M.G.H.* N.S. **4**, 1884, 221-5. 18-19th c.

Dickens
RUST, DOUGLAS. 'Charles Dickens and his local connections', *W.M.* **13**(2), 1995, 11-18. Concerns Dickens, Cooper and Mitton families.

Dilke
See Finch

Dodd
See Portales

Dolben
See Myddelton

Dolins
See Boddington

Doubleday
CAMERON, ANDREA, & YARDE, DORIS. 'The Doubledays of St.Mary's, Spring Grove', *Honeslaw chronicle* **11**(2), 1988, 1821, **12**(1), 1989, 15-18. 19th c.

Dove
BRAITHWAITE, DAVID. *Building in the blood: the story of Dove Brothers of Islington, 1781-1981.* Godfrey Cave Associates, 1981.

Draper
'The family of Draper', *Reliquary* **15**, 1874-5, 192. Pedigree, 18-19th c.

Druce
DRUCE, C. *A genealogical account of the family of Druce of Goreing in the county of Oxon, and those of kin to the children of George Druce, citizen and painter-stainer of the parish of All Saints, Breadstreet, in the City of London, by whom this genealogy was taken ...* [ ], 1735. 17-18th c.

Drummond
BOLITHO, HECTOR, & PEEL, DEREK. *The Drummonds of Charing Cross.* Allen & Unwin, 1967.
BOLITHO, HECTOR. 'The house of Drummond', *Three banks review* **75**, 1967, 33-41. 18th c.

Du Prie
FERGUSON, T. COLYER. 'Pedigree of the family of Du Prie', *M.G.H.* 3rd series **5**, 1904, 81-3. 17th c.

Du Toict
DUTHOIT, J.F. 'The family of Du Toict, Du Toit, or Duthoit', *Pr.Hug.Soc.L.* **14**, 1930-33, 589-94. Of Kent and London; includes folded pedigree, 17-19th c.

Dugdale
'Dugdale', *Genealogist* **4**, 1880, 124-5. Extracts from parish registers of St.Lawrence Jewry, *etc.,* 18th c.

Duke
DUKE, RASHLEIGH E.H. 'Parentage of Richard Duke the poet', *M.G.H.* 5th series **1**, 1916, 33-5. Pedigree, 17-18th c., with extracts from family bible.

Duprat de Charreau
WAGNER, HENRY. 'A study of the Huguenot refugee families of Duprat de Charreau, and Maseres', *Genealogist* N.S. **24**, 1908, 264-5. 18th c.

Dupuis
BULLOCK-WEBSTER, A. 'The Dupuis family',
Pr.Hug.Soc.L. **2**, 1887-8, 162-5. Of London,
Surrey and Oxfordshire, *etc.*
WAGNER, HENRY. 'Huguenot refugee family
of Dupuis', *M.G.H.* N.S. **3**, 1880, 249-51.
18-19th c.

Duroure
WAGNER, HENRY. 'The English branch of
Duroure', *Pr.Hug.Soc.L.* **10**, 1912-14,
399-400. Folded pedigree, 17-19th c.

Dutens
WAGNER, HENRY. 'Pedigreee of the family of
Dutens', *M.G.H.* 4th series **1**, 1906, 233-5.
Of The Hague, London, *etc.,* 18-19th c.

Duthoit
See Du Toict

Dutilh
WAGNER, HENRY. 'Pedigree of Dutilh *alias*
Rigaud', *M.G.H.* 3rd series **3**, 1900, 24.
France and London; 18th c.

Dwight
CHURCH, ARTHUR H., SIR. 'The family of
John Dwight, B.C.L., potter', *Genealogist*
N.S. **27**, 1911, 74-77. Includes pedigree,
15-18th c.

Dyos
LLOYD, HILARY. 'The Dyos family of
Laleham', *W.M.* **8**(3), 1990, 85-7. 19th c.

Edwards
ROUND, J.H. 'Pedigree of Edwards (London
visitation of 1634)', *Genealogist* N.S. **10**,
1894, 183-5. 17-18th c.
SMITH, ELIZUR YALE. 'The English ancestry
of Jonathon Edwards, *New York
genealogical and biographical record* **70**,
1939, 104-10. 16th c.

Egg
BLAIR, CLAUDE. 'The Egg family', *Arms and
Armour Society journal* **7**, 1973, 266-99 &
305-53. 18-19th c.

Eldred
S[TEINMAN], G.S. 'Genealogical notes of the
Eldred family', *C.T.G.* **6**, 1840, 295-7. Of
Essex and London, 17-18th c.

Ellicott
FOULKES, ROBERT K. 'The Ellicotts: a family
of clockmakers', *Antiquarian horology* **3**,
1959-62, 102-10.

Elliot
PEARCE, K.R. 'The Elliot family', *J.H.H.L.H.S.*
21, 1980, 11-12. 19th c.

Elsom
WOODGATE, MARY. 'A metropolitan family',
N.M. **15**(3), 1993, 99-102. Elsom family, 18-
19th c.

Elwes
'Elwes', *M.G.H.* **1**, 1868, 71. Parish register
extracts from London and
Nottinghamshire, *etc.,* 16-18th c.

Erith
ERITH, E.J. 'An East London business', *East
London record* **17**, 1994-5, 28-34. Erith
family business, 19th c.

Essington
'Essington', *M.G.H.* 5th series **5**, 1923-5,
326-9. Of London and Surrey; pedigree,
17-18th c., with wills.

Eude
HOOD, JAMES W. 'Eude to Hood', *Proceedings
of the Huguenot Society of London* **23**,
1979, 187-92. 17-18th c.

Evans
WEBSTER, ANGELA. 'Evans families in
Bethnal Green', *C.A.* **20**, 1983, 20-22.
19th c.

Evatt
WHITMORE, J.B. 'Pedigree of Evatt',
M.G.H. 5th series **7**, 1929-31, 145-9.
16-19th c.

Evelyn
'Evelyn of Harrow on the Hill', *M.G.H.* 2nd
series **4**, 1892, 296-7. 15-16th c.

Exelby
BARRON, OSWALD. 'The gentility of William
Exelby', *Ancestor* **3**, Oct 1902, 127-31. 16-
17th c.

ESHELBY, H.D. 'Notes on the genealogy of Exelby of London, Herts, &c', *Genealogist* N.S. **10**, 1894, 20-28, 116-22 & 14655. Includes pedigree, 16-19th c.

Fabian
BOYD, P. 'A fighting draper', *Genealogists' magazine* **7**, 1935-7, 10-11. Fabian family, 15th c.

Fanshawe
'Fanshawe pedigree', *M.G.H.* **1**, 1868, 320-21. 16-17th c.
'Fanshawe', *M.G.H.* **2**, 1876, 4-15. Extracts from parish registers, 16-19th c.

Farnell
YARDE, D.M. 'The Farnell brothers', *Honeslaw chronicle* **14**, 1991, 16-22. 19th c.

Farrington
See Morton

Farthing
'John Farthing of Perivale', *Local historian [Ealing Local History Society]* **3**, 1963, 31-2 & 36-7. Includes notes on family, 17-19th c.

Fassnidge/Fastnedge
FASSNEDGE, JOHN. 'Skilled craftsmen made good', *H.F.H.S.M.* **35**, 1996, 13-16. Fassnidge or Fastnedge family, of Great Missenden and Uxbridge. 19-20th c., includes pedigree.

Fauquier
WOLLASTON, G. WOODS. 'The family of Fauquier', *Pr.Hug.Soc.L.* **13**, 1923-9, 340-55. 17-19th c., includes pedigree.

Fearn
See Nicholas

Fell
SCHOMBERG, ARTHUR. 'Fell', *M.G.H.* 2nd series **2**, 1888, 288. Pedigree, 18th c.

Ferard
'Pedigree of the Huguenot refugee family of Ferard', *M.G.H.* 4th series **2**, 1908, 90-92. 18-20th c.

Ferguson
BODDINGTON, REGINALD STEWART. 'Ferguson and Berry', *M.G.H.* N.S. **4**, 1884, 213. Pedigree, 18-19th c.

Ferrers
FERRERS, CECIL S.F. 'Pedigree of the Berkshire and London branch of the Ferrers family, as compiled by Sir Edward Wilson, Bart., (1752), Edmund Ferrers, F.S.A., rector of Cheriton, Hants., (1806-1825) and other later members of the family', *Genealogist* N.S. **27**, 1911, 24-6. 17-19th c.

Fettiplace
DUNLOP, J. RENTON. 'Pedigree of the Fettiplace family of London and Essex', *M.G.H.* 5th series **6**, 1926-8, 68-71. 16-18th c.

Field
FIELD, OSGOOD. 'Matthew Field of London, mercer: his family and arms', *N.E.H.G.R.* **48**, 1895, 331-6. 16-17th c.

Finch
'Finch, Fisher, Throckmorton and Dilke families', *M.G.H.* 2nd series **3**, 1890, 108-10. From family bibles, *etc.,* 17-18th c.
'Finch', *M.G.H.* 5th series **9**, 1935-7, 266-7. Pedigree, 17th c.

Fisher
See Finch

Fitzhugh
See Brown

Fitzwalter
WILMOTT, TONY. 'The arms of Fitzwalter on leather scabbards from London', *T.L.M.A.S.* **32**, 1981, 132-9. Includes medieval pedigree.

Flack
BENTON, TONY. 'The Flacks and marriage', *N.M.* **6**(1), 1983, 26-7. Flack family, 18-19th c.

Fleetwood

BUSS, ROBERT WOODWARD. *Fleetwood family records.* Privately printed, 1920. Of Lancashire and various other counties; many pedigrees, including that of Fleetwood of Wood Street, Cheapside, 18-19th c.

SHIRREEN, A.J. 'The Fleetwoods of Ealing and Cranford', *Notes and queries* **198**, 1953, 7-14. 16-17th c.

Forsett

SMITH, G.C. MOORE. 'Forsett of Marylebone and Wells Hall, Co.Suffolk', *Genealogist* N.S. **21**, 1905, 106-13. Pedigree, 16-17th c.

Forster

COMPTON, THEODORE. *Recollections of Tottenham friends and the Forster family.* Edward Hicks, 1893. 18-19th c.

Fowler

WATERS, EDMOND CHESTER. 'Pedigree of Fowler of Barnsbury, Co.Middlesex', *Herald and genealogist* **7**, 1873, 559-60. 16-17th c.

Fox

ADAMS, G.E. 'Genealogical memoranda relating to the Fox and Weld families', *M.G.H.* N.S. **1**, 1874, 113-4. Includes pedigree, 17-18th c.

GANDELL, H.L. 'The Holland baronies', *Coat of arms* **10** 19689, 276. Fox family, 17-18th c.

ILCHESTER, EARL OF. *The home of the Hollands, 1605-1820.* Murray, 1937.

ILCHESTER, EARL OF. *Chronicles of Holland House, 1820-1900.* John Murray, 1937. Fox family, Lords Holland.

SMITH, J. CHALLENOR. 'The families of Fox and Tattershall', *Genealogist* N.S. **30**, 1914, 150-3. Of Middlesex and Hampshire; 16th c.

Franklin

FRANKLIN, ARTHUR ELLIS. *Records of the Franklin family and collaterals.* 2nd ed. George Roulledge & Sons, 1935. 18-20th c.

Frederick

ROBINSON, C.J. 'Notes relating to the family of Frederick', *M.G.H.* N.S. **1**, 1874, 410. Extracts from the parish register of St.Olave Old Jewry, 17-18th c.

SUCKLING, F.H. *The family of Frederick of Frederick Place, Old Jewry, London, and of Bampton, Oxon.* Exeter: William Pollard, 1911. 17-18th c.

SUCKLING, F.H. 'The family of Frederick, of Frederick Place, Old Jewry, London', *Genealogist* N.S. **27**, 1911, 65-73 & 14953. 17-18th c.

'Frederick', *M.G.H.* 3rd series **2**, 1898, 134. Of London and Walton on Thames, Surrey; from family bible, 18th c.

Freeman

FREEMAN, JESSICA. 'Migrating ancestors: into London and out again', *N.M.* **7**(4), 1985, 124-6. Freeman family, 16-18th c., of London, Northamptonshire, *etc.*

Fremeaux

See Rickard

Freshfield

FLINN, JUDY. *A history of Freshfields.* Freshfields, 1984. City solicitors; includes much information on the Freshfield family, also list of partners, 1716-1983.

Fressh

THRELFALL, JOHN B. 'John Fressh, Lord Mayor of London in 1395: a study in medieval genealogy', *Genealogists' magazine* **21**, 1983-5, 289-93, 321-4, 350-55 & 396-7. Includes will, 1397.

Frogmore

ZOUCH, CONNIE. 'Frogmore Farm', *W.M.* **10**(1), 1992, 27-33. Includes pedigree of Frogmore, 17th c.

Frost

DODDERIDGE, S.E. 'Pedigree of Frost of Bishopsgate, London', *M.G.H.* 4th series **5**, 1913, 364-5. 19-20th c.

Fuller

FULLER, J.F. 'De Ffulwer or Ffuller pedigree', *M.G.H.* 4th series **4**, 1911, 30-5 & 66-70. Of Essex, London, *etc.,* medieval-17th c.

FULLER, JAMES FRANKLIN. 'Fuller family', *M.G.H.* **1**, 1868, 214-5. See also 288. Of London and Ireland; includes undated pedigree.

Furness
DALL, CAROLINE H. 'The Furness pedigree'. *N.E.H.G.R.* **30**, 1870, 63-4. Of London, undated.

Fysh
FYSH, J.P.G., & FYSH, A.V.G.A. 'A Fysh family in London and further afield', *Norfolk ancestor* **2**(1), 1980, 3-9. 19-20th c.

Galliard
'Galliard and Huxley entries from Edmonton registers', *M.G.H.* 2nd series **1**, 1886, 198. 17-18th c.

Gardner
See James

Garnault
WAGNER, HENRY. 'Pedigree of Garnault', *Pr.Hug.Soc.L.* **11**, 1915-17, 149-51. Folded pedigree, 17-19th c.

Gayfer
BODDINGTON, REGINALD STEWART. 'Pedigree of the family of Gayfer', *M.G.H.* 2nd series **4**, 1892, 201-2. Of Suffolk and Middlesex; 17-19th c.

Gayre
GAYRE, GEORGE ROBERT, & GAIR, R.L. *Gayre's booke, being a history of the family of Gayre. Vol.IV.* Edinburgh: Oliver & Boyd, 1959. Includes pedigrees of the Gayres in London, SouthWest England, *etc*.

Gee
WILSON, SHEILA. 'The Gees of Fenton House', *C.H.R.* **19**, 1995, 10-12. In Hampstead, 18th c.

Gervaise
WAGNER, HENRY. 'Gervaise', *M.G.H.* 3rd series **2**, 1898, 59. 17-18th c.

Gery
CULLUM, GERY MILNER GIBSON. 'Pedigree of Gery of Great Ealing, Middlesex', *M.G.H.* 4th series **2**, 1908, 113. 17-18th c.

Gibbins
See Gillett

Gibbs
GIBBS, JOHN ARTHUR. *The history of Antony and Dorothea Gibbs and of their contemporary relatives, including the history of the origin & early years of the house of Antony Gibbs and Sons.* Saint Catherine Press, 1922. Of Exeter and London, 18-19th c. Includes folded pedigrees of Gibbs, Hucks of Hertfordshire, and Crawley.

Gideon
KANDEL, EDWARD M. 'The ancestors and descendants of Sampson Gideon', *Coat of arms* N.S., **2** (102), 1977, 153-6 & 171. Includes pedigree, 17-20th c.

Gieves
GIEVE, DAVID W. *Gieves and Hawkes 1785-1985: the story of a tradition.* Gieves & Hawkes Ltd., 1985. History of a firm of tailors; includes pedigree of Gieves, 18-20th c., also list of long serving staff.

Gilbert
See Boulier and Grace

Gilbey
WAUGH, ALEC. *Merchants of wine, being a centenary account of the fortunes of the house of Gilbey.* Cassell & Co., 1957. Includes pedigree of Gilbey family, 18-20th c.

Gill
'Gill pedigree', *M.G.H.* **2**, 1876, 24-32. Of Hertfordshire and London, *etc.*, 15-19th c.

Gillett
SAYERS, R.S. *Gilletts in the London money market, 1867-1967.* Oxford: Clarendon Press, 1968. Includes folded pedigree of Gibbins and Gillett, 18-20th c.

Gillman
GILLMAN, ALEXANDER W. *The Gillmans of Highgate, with letters from Samuel Taylor Coleridge, &c., being a chapter from the history of the Gilman family.* Elliot Stock, 1895. 18-19th c.

GILLMAN, ALEXANDER WILLIAM. *Searches into the history of the Gillman or Gilman family, including the various brances of England, Ireland, America and Belgium.* Elliot Stock, 1895. Includes chapters on the family in Wales, London, Surrey, Ireland, Hertfordshire and Essex, Gloucestershire, Kent, Norfolk, *etc., etc.,* with folded pedigrees , medieval-19th c.

Glover
EXCELL, STANLEY. 'Family history from a modern mug', *N.M.* **8**, 1986, 63-6. Glover family, 19th c.

Glyn
FULFORD, ROGER. *Glyn's, 1753-1953: six generations in Lombard Street.* Macmillan, 1953. A banking family.

Godde
'Memoranda relating to the (?) French refugee family of Godde', *M.G.H.* N.S. **3**, 1880, 221-2. Pedigree, 18-19th c.

Godfrey
See Hankwitz

Godin
CARMICHAEL, EVELYN G.M. 'Family note book of Stephen Peter Godin', *Genealogist* N.S. **28**, 1912, 129-41. 18th c.

Golden
See Saunders

Goldsmid
HYAMSON, ALBERT M. 'An Anglo-Jewish family', *The Jewish Historical Society of England transactions* **17**, 1951-2, 1-10. Goldsmid family; includes pedigrees, 18-20th c.

Golightly
See Portales

Gonson
See Gunson

Goodday
'Memoranda relating to the family of Goodday, Co.Middlesex and Suffolk', *Genealogist* **3**, 1879, 51-3. Extracts from parish registers, *etc.,* 17-18th c.

Gore
HOWLAND, McCLURE MEREDITH. 'English background of three New England families', *N.E.H.G.R.* **115**, 1961, 253-6. Gore, Cheever and Cole (Lobel) families, 17th c.
'Annotations to the heraldic visitation of London, 1633: Gore', *M.G.H.* 2nd series **3**, 1890, 71-2, 116-8 & 151-3. Includes parish register extracts.

Gorges
MACLEAN, JOHN. 'Gorges family, Chelsea', *Western antiquary* **1**, 1881, 102. Monumental inscription, 1668; includes 17th c. baptisms.

Gorsuch
GORSUCH, D. 'Miracles do happen', *C.A.* **49**, 1990-91, 22-5. Gorsuch family; includes pedigree, 19-20th c.

Gorton
See Maplett

Gosset
GOSSET, MARY H. 'A family of modellers in wax', *Pr.Hug.Soc.L.* **3**, 1888-91, 541-68. Gosset family; includes folded pedigrees, 18-19th c.

Gould
'Pedigree of the family of Gould', *M.G.H.* N.S. **3**, 1880, 3558. 17-19th c.

Gouthit
See Skilbeck

Grace
'Cricketers at Goodenough House', *Local historian [Ealing Local History Society]* 3(2), 1963, 29-30. South Ealing; Grace and Gilbert families, 19-20th c.

Graham
See Portales

Grant
'Genealogical memoranda relating to the Grant family', *M.G.H.* N.S. **1**, 1874, 216. Notes from a prayer book, early 18th c.

Gray

CROUCH, CHARLES HALL. 'Ancestry of Thomas Gray the poet', *Genealogists' magazine* **3**(4), 1927, 74-8. Includes pedigree, 17-18th c.

HEWLETT, GEOFFREY. 'The Gray family of Wembley Park', *W.H.S.J.* **6**(2), 1986, 26-33. 18-19th c.

HONAN, ROBERT F. *The Gray matter: the Gray family history, 16th to 20th century* ... Adelaide: Lutheran Publishing House, 1987. Of Berkshire, Hampshire, Oxfordshire, London, Middlesex, Suffolk and Australia. Includes pedigrees.

See also Boddington

Grazebrook

GRAZEBROOK, GEO. 'Descent in the male line of the family of Grazebrook from 1065, with proofs for each generation', *M.G.H.* 4th series **2**, 1908, 268-73 & 311-16; 4th series **3**, 1910, 1826, 77-85, 106-13, 150-57, 198-203, 254-61, 305-12 & 366-70; 4th series **4**, 1911, 1-7, 56-9 & 126-33. See also 92-4 & 140-42. Medieval; of Staffordshire and London, *etc.,* includes various extracts from primary sources.

Greenwell

'Greenwell family', *M.G.H.* N.S. **2**, 1877, 396-7. Extracts from family bible and monumental inscriptions, 18-19th c.

Gregson

PRINDLE, PAUL W. 'English ancestry of Thomas Gregson of New Haven', *N.E.H.G.R.* **127** 1973, 167-77 & 260-67; **128** 1974, 6573 & 106-12. Of Derbyshire and London, 16-17th c; includes wills and extracts from Sutton on the Hill parish register.

Gresham

GOWER, GRANVILLE LEVESON. *Genealogy of the family of Gresham.* Mitchell & Hughes, 1883.

GOWER, GRANVILLE LEVESON. 'Genealogical memoranda relating to the Gresham family', *M.G.H.* **2**, 1876, 311-16. Of Norfolk and London; grants of arms and pedigrees, 15-17th c.

'Births of the children of Sir John Gresham, Lord Mayor of London in 1547, by his first wife Mary, daughter and co-heir of Thomas Ipswell', *Topographer and genealogist* **2**, 1853, 512-4.

'Gresham memoranda', *M.G.H.* 2nd series **3**, 1890, 195-6. 17th c.

'Pedigree of Gresham: issue of Edward Gresham', *M.G.H.* N.S. **4**, 1884, 301-8. 17-18th c.

See also Roe

Grimsdale

PEARCE, K.R. 'Grimsdale and Sons', *U.R.* **31**, 1979, 5-9. Includes pedigree, 18-20th c.

Grosvenor

CHATER, MICHAEL. *Family business: a history of Grosvenor Chater, 1690-1977.* St. Albans: Grosvenor Chater, 1977. Includes pedigrees of Grosvenor, Chater and Rutt.

SHEPPARD, FRANCIS. 'The Grosvenor estate, 1677-1977', *History today* **27**, 1977, 726-33.

See also Davies

Grover

WHITTLETON, ERIC H. *The Grover family of Ealing.* Ealing Museum, Art & History Society, 1982. Includes pedigree, 18-19th c.

See also Deacon

Guinand

WAGNER, HENRY. 'Pedigree of Guinand', *M.G.H.* 4th series **4**, 1911, 270-71. 18-19th c.

Gumley

LANG, M.E. 'The Gumley family', *Honeslaw chronicle* **4**(2), 1981, 14-16. 18th c.

Gunson

GUNSON, W.M. 'The family of Gunson or Gonson of London and Essex', *Family history* **8**(46); N.S. **22/23**, 1974, 133-46. 1617th c.

Hadfield

See Rickard

Haines

'Haines', *M.G.H.* 2nd series **3**, 1890, 38-40. Of Hackney, *etc.,* pedigree, 17th c., with inquisitions post mortem, *etc.*

Haldimand
WAGNER, HENRY. 'Fragmentary pedigree of Haldimand and Marcet', *M.G.H.* N.S. **4**, 1884, 369-70. 18-19th c.

Hall
DOBSON, CHARLES GEORGE. *A century and a quarter: the story of the growth of our business from 1824 to the present day.* Hall & Co., 1951. History of Hall & Co., coal factors and builders' merchants. Includes Hall family pedigree, 18-20th c.

HALL, H.F. 'Hall pedigrees', *M.G.H.* **2**, 1876, 255-6. 17th c.

MARSHALL, GEORGE W. 'Family of Hall: additions to the visitation of London ...', no.III', *M.G.H.* N.S. **1**, 1874, 12731 & 457-76. Extracts from parish registers of St.Nicholas Acon, London, Gravesend, Kent, and Bengeo, Hertfordshire, *etc.,* monumental inscriptions from Bengeo and Sutton, Surrey; many Hall wills, also will of Sir Martin Lumley of London, 1631; pedigrees of Lumley of London and Great Bardfield, Essex, 17th c., Hall of Horsham, Sussex and London, and Ravenscroft of Horsham, 16-17th c., Hall of Worcestershire, 17th c.

Halley
MCPIKE, EUGENE F. 'Some material for a pedigree of Dr. Edmond Halley', *Genealogist* N.S. **25**, 1909, 5-14. See also 143-4, 207 & 271-2; **34**, 1918, 116. 17th c. Includes wills.

Hamey
KEEVIL, JOHN. 'The Hameys in the Netherlands, Russia, London and Chelsea, 1568-1676', *Pr.Hug.Soc.L.* **19**(1), 1953, 26-55. Includes pedigree.

Hamilton
HARWOOD, H.W. FORSYTH. 'The genealogy of the family of Hamilton of Ypres in Flanders, and afterwards of London', *Genealogist* N.S. **14**, 1898, 264-71. 17-18th c.

Hammond
BURNBY, J.G.L. *The Hammonds of Edmonton.* Occasional paper N.S. **26**. E.H.H.S., 1973. Includes pedigree, 18-19th c.

Hanbury
LOCKE, A. AUDREY. *The Hanbury family.* 2 vols. Arthur L. Humphreys, 1916. Of Worcestershire, London, *etc.* Includes pedigrees, 12-20th c.

Hanckwitz
WAGNER, HENRY. 'A tentative pedigree of Hanckwitz, known later as Godfrey', *Genealogist* N.S. **26**, 1910, 244-5. See also 62-3. 18th c.

Hanson
GOODWIN, GEORGE. *Hansons of Eastcheap: the story of the house of Samuel Hanson and Son, Ltd., 1747-1947.* Saml. Hanson & Son, 1947.

Harman
BRADNEY, JOSEPH. 'Harman', *M.G.H.* 5th series **7**, 1929-31, 223. Of Soho; brief pedigree, 17-18th c.

Harrap
'Journeymen coopers from Wapping', *C.A.* **7**, 1980, 6-7. Harrap family; 19-20th c.

Harris
COLLINS, TINDALL. *Richard and the Square Mile: a short history (1610-1815) of the Harris family, Quakers, mercers and cornfactors, of Fordingbridge and the City of London.* Salisbury: Jill Bullen, 1983. Includes pedigree.

Harvey
HARVEY, WILLIAM J. *Genealogy of the family of Harvey, of Folkestone, Co.Kent, London, Hackney and Twickenham, Co.Middlesex; Croydon, Putney and Kingston, Co.Surrey; Hempstead, Chigwell and Barking, Co.Essex; Clifton and Wike, Co.Dorset, etc.* Mitchell & Hughes, 1889. Pedigrees, 16-19th c.

HARRIS, DAVID ALEXANDER. 'A Jewish family in the East End: Harris', *C.A.* **74**, 1997, 41-2. 19-20th c.

Hatchard
HUMPHREYS, ARTHUR L. *Piccadilly bookmen: memorials of the house of Hatchard.* Hatchards, 1893. Includes outline pedigree, 18-19th c., obituary notices, *etc.*

Hawkes
See Gieves

Hawtrey
HAWTREY, FLORENCE MOLESWORTH. *The history of the Hawtrey family.* 2 vols. George Allen, 1903. Of Chequers, Ruislip, *etc.* includes pedigree, medieval-19th c.

Haydock
MURRAY, B. 'A martyr in the family', *Catholic ancestor* 4(2), 1992, 74-5. Line pedigree shewing descent from Haydock to Shuttleworth, Creamor, *etc.,* 17-20th c. Of Lancashire, Nottinghamshire and London.

Haynes
COX, A.H. 'A genius and his family', *W.D.D.H.* 51, 1975, 36. Haynes family, 18-20th c.
WAGNER, HENRY. 'The descendants of Hopton Haynes', *Genealogist* N.S. 20, 1904, 280-81. Pedigree, 17-18th c.

Hazlitt
HAZLITT, WILLIAM CAREW. *The Hazlitts: an account of their origin and descent, with autobiographical particulars of William Hazlitt (1778-1830), notices of his relatives and immediate posterity, and a series of illustrative letters. (1772-1865).* Edinburgh: Ballantyne Hanson & Co., 1911. 18-19th c.
HAZLITT, WILLIAM CAREW. *The Hazlitts, part the second: a narrative of the later fortunes of the family, with a survey of the western and other suburbs of London as they were sixty years since.* Edinburgh: Ballantyne, Hanson & Co., 1912. 19th c.

Hearne
HEARNE, JACK. 'The cricketer Hearnes of Middlesex, M.C.C., and England', *J.H.H.L.H.S.* 41, 1990, 6-10. 19-20th c.
HEARNE, JACK. 'An eleven of Hearnes', *W.M.* 7(1), 1988, 2021. Includes pedigree, 19-20th c.
See also Jenks

Heath
See Brown

Heathcote
'Heathcote of Chesterfield, Lord Mayor of London', *Reliquary* 2, 1881-2, 156. Pedigreee, 18th c.

Heaton
SKEAT, FRANCIS. 'Heaton, Butler and Bayne: a famous Victorian firm', *Family history* 10(69-70); N.S., 45/46, 1979, 231-50. 19-20th c.

Hempstead
BURGESS, RITA C. 'Hempstead of Suffolk and Middlesex', *Suffolk roots: the journal of the Suffolk Genealogy Society* 13(4), 1987, 88-90; 14(1), 1988, 16-17; 14(2), 1988, 48. 19th c.

Henley
CURRIE, ANN. *Henleys of Wapping: a London shipowning family, 1770-1830.* Maritime monographs & reports 62. National Maritime Museum, 1988. Includes pedigree.
VILLE, SIMON P. *English shipowning during the Industrial Revolution: Michael Henley and Son, London, shipowners, 1770-1830.* Manchester: Manchester University Press, 1987.

Herridge
MOWAT, P. 'The Herridge saga', *Greentrees: the journal of the Westminster and Central Middlesex Family History Society* 14(2), 1995, 36-7. 19th c.

Heyron
REDSTONE, VINCENT B., & REDSTONE, LILIAN J.A. 'The Heyrons of London: a study in the social origins of Geoffrey Chaucer', *Speculum* 12, 1937, 182-95. 14-15th c.

Hill
See Brown

Hinton
'Hinton pedigree', *M.G.H.* N.S. 4, 1884, 148. Of Staffordshire, Warwickshire, and London; 17th c.

Hoare

HOARE, EDWARD. 'The annals of Hoare's Bank', *Genealogists' magazine* **7**, 1935-7, 288-98. Hoare family, 17-19th c.

TYLER, BRENDA. 'The Hoares of Hampstead', *C.H.R.* **3**, 1975, 9-10. 18-19th c.

See also Hore

Hodilow

B., W.D. 'An account of the family of Hodilow of Cambridgeshire, Essex, Northamptonshire and Middlesex', *Topographer and genealogist* **2**, 1853, 28-72. 15-17th c.

Holford

MACQUEEN, FELICITY. 'The Holfords of Hampstead: the story of a leading local family', *C.H.R.* **6**, 1978, 12-13. 18-19th c.

See also Boddington

Holland

See Fox

Hollis

WHITLEY, W.T. 'The Hollis family and Pinners Hall', *Baptist quarterly* **1**, 1922, 78-81. Brief note, 17th c., of Yorkshire and London.

Holwell

GEARE, R. HOLWELL. 'An old family associated with City companies', *Notes and queries* **209**; N.S. **11**, 1964, 42-4. Holwell family, 14-17th c.

Hood

See Eude

Horde

See Roberts

Hore

HOARE, EDWARD. *Some account of the early history and genealogy, with pedigrees from 1330, unbroken to the present time, of the families of Hore and Hoare, with all their branches ...* Alfred Russell Smith, 1883. Of Devon, London and various other counties.

Horton

ANDERSON, ROBERT CHARLES. 'The Conant connection, part one: Thomas Horton, London merchant and father-in-law of Roger Conant', *N.E.H.G.R.* **147**, 1993, 234-9 Horton family, 16-17th c; includes wills.

Horton-Smith

See Saunders

Hotton

GREGG, DANIELLE C. 'A change of name in a Middlesex family', *Metropolitan* **18**(2), 1995, 60-62. Hotton *als* Orten family, early 19th c.

Houblon

HOUBLON, ALICE F.A. *The Houblon family: its story and times.* 2 vols. Archibald Constable, 1907. Of France, London and Essex; includes pedigrees, 16-19th c.

Howard

BRADBROOKE, WILLIAM. 'Howard', *M.G.H.* 3rd series **4**, 1902, 191-5. Extracts from parish registers of Bethnal Green, Middlesex, and Cobham, Surrey, 17-19th c.

FISKE, R.C. 'The Howards of Brockdish and Hackney', *Norfolk ancestor* 1(3), 1978, 33-5. Pedigree, 15-18th c. Brockdish, Norfolk.

WATSON, ROWLAND. *The house of Howard: the story of an English firm.* Country Life, 1952. 19-20th c.

Hucks

See Gibbs

Hunnings

FOSTER, W.E. *Some notes on the families of Hunnings of South Lincolnshire, London and Suffolk.* Exeter: William Pollard, 1912. Supplement to *Genealogist* N.S. **28-9**. Includes pedigrees, 1319th c.

Hunt

TATCHELL, MOLLY. *Leigh Hunt and his family in Hammersmith.* Hammersmith Local History Group, 1969. 19th c.

Hurlock

BURCH, DOROTHY. *Hurlocks of London, 17th to 20th centuries.* Leicester: the author, 1995. Includes pedigrees.

BURCH, DOROTHY. 'Hurlocks of London – or elsewhere?', *C.A.* **68**, 1995, 46-7. 18th c.

Huxley
See Galliard

Hyde
CAMPBELL, STELLA M. 'The Hyde family and York House, Twickenham', *Middlesex Local History Council bulletin* **6**, 1958, 1-6. 17th c.

Ingle
WRIGHT, FRED. 'The Ingles of Limehouse', *East London record* **15**, 1992, 15-21. Ingle family, 19th c.

Ipswell
See Gresham

Irons
CAPEWELL, JANICE. 'The search for a mariner', *Midland ancestor* **4**, 1977, 267-9. Irons family of Mile End.

Jackson
RAVEN, C.R. 'Jackson family bible', *N.M.* **4**(2), 1981/2, 91. Brief entries, 1860-1913. Hackney and Bethnal Green mentioned.
WAGNER, HENRY. 'Jackson of London', *M.G.H.* N.S. **4**, 1884, 74-5. 18th c.

James
C., R.C. 'Family of James, of London, Essex, Kent, Suffolk and Surrey', *East Anglian* **1**, 1858-63, 330-31. 16-19th c.
JAMES, E. RENOUARD. *Genealogical notes on the descent of James of Austin Friars.* [ ], 1898. Includes folded pedigrees; also pedigrees of Renouard, Ott and Gardner, medieval-19th c.
See also Barefoot

Jenks
COLKET, MEREDITH. 'The Jenks family of England', *N.E.H.G.R.* **110**, 1956, 9-20, 81-93, 161-72 & 244-56. 16-17th c; includes wills, parish register extracts, *etc;* also includes notes on Hearne of Buckinghamshire.
COLKET, MEREDITH. 'The father of Joseph Jenks of Lynn: a proposed solution to an intriguing genealogical puzzle', *N.E.H.G.R.* **122**, 1968, 168-71. 17th c. Lynn, Massachusetts.

Johnson
MCDONALD, DONALD. *The Johnsons of Maiden Lane.* Martins, 1964. 18-20th c.
'Found in a bible in a London bookshop', *N.M.* **2**(3), 1980, 110-11. Entries relating to Johnson family, 1817-1949.

Jollit
WAGNER, HENRY. 'Pedigree of the Huguenot refugee family of Jollit or Jolit', *M.G.H.* 4th series **3**, 1910, 182-3. 18-19th c.

Keadall
ADAMS, JEFF. 'The Keadalls in Brentford', *W.M.* **4**(4), 1984, 103-7. 18-20th c.

Keling
F[LETCHER], W.G.D. 'The family of Keling or Kelynge', *Reliquary* **24**, 1883-4, 47-8. Of Bedfordshire and London. 17th c. pedigree, with wills.

Kemp(e)
CARSE, VENETIA, & HUGHES, DOROTHEA. *A family history of the Kempes.* []: [privately published], 1992. 19-20th c.
HITCHIN-KEMP, FRED. *A general history of the Kemp and Kempe families of Great Britain and her colonies* ... Leadenhall Press, 1902. Of Kent, Norfolk, Suffolk, Essex, Middlesex, Cornwall, Sussex, *etc.* Includes pedigrees, medieval-19th c.
KEMPE, JOHN. *A family history of the Kempes.* Stanford: Peter Spiegl & Co., 1991. Of Cornwall, London, Australia, *etc.,* medieval-20th c.

Kingsley
PINK, W.D. 'Kingsley of Sarratt, Canterbury, and London', *Genealogist* N.S. **29**, 1913, 212-24, & **30**, 1914, 35-8 & 86-94. Sarratt, Hertfordshire, and Canterbury, Kent; 16-19th c., includes wills.

Kitchell
'Kitchell', *M.G.H.* N.S. **4**, 1884, 398-400 & 405-7. Of London and Kent; 17th c. pedigrees, wills and monumental inscriptions.

Knevett
See Warner

Knibb
LEE, RONALD A. 'The Knibb family,
clockmakers', *Antiquarian horology* **4**,
1962-5, 202-9 & 232-9. Of London and
Oxford.

Knollys
JONES, THOMAS WHARTON. 'Inquiry into
the early history of the family of Sir
Francis Knollys, K.G., P.C., and treasurer
of the household to Queen Elizabeth',
Herald and genealogist **7**, 1873, 553-60. 15-
17th c.

Knowles
C[OKAYNE], G.E. 'Pedigree of Knowles of
London', *Genealogist* N.S. **18**, 1902, 225-
30. 17th c., includes extracts from parish
registers, and wills.

La Primaudaye
WAGNER, HENRY. 'The Huguenot refugee
family of La Primaudaye', *Genealogist*
N.S. **23**, 1907, 171-3. 18-19th c.

Lacaux
WAGNER, HENRY. 'Pedigree of the Huguenot
refugee family of Lacaux', *Genealogist*
N.S. **25**, 1909, 246-7. 18th c.

Lacy
'The Lacy family tree', *H.F.H.S.M.* **2**, 1988,
18. Pedigree, 19-20th c.

Lancashire
BARBER-LOMAX, J.W. 'A Lancashire family in
London', *Lancashire [Rossendale Society
for Genealogy & Heraldry journal]* **4**(3),
1983, 17-19. 17th c.

Lane
'Pedigree of Lane from visitation of London,
1687, in College of Arms', *M.G.H.* N.S. **1**,
1874, 186-7.
See also Brown

Lavender
HANNINGTON, VALERIE. 'Local families, no.1:
Lavender', *H.F.H.S.M.* **1**, 1988, 5-6.
Includes pedigree, 18-19th c.
See also Lawrence

Lawrence
SPINK, KAREN. 'Field End: a glimpse at life
in the 19th century', *R.N.E.,* April 1987,
37-40. Ruislip; includes pedigree showing
relationship of Lawrence, Lavender and
Powell, 18-20th c.
'Lawrence of London', *M.G.H.* **1**, 1868, 243.
17th c. pedigree.

Layard
WAGNER, HENRY. 'Notes on the pedigree of
Layard', *Pr.Hug.Soc.L.* **9**, 1909-11, 254-6.
Includes folded pedigree, 17-19th c.

Layton
'Layton', *M.G.H.* **1**, 1868, 256. London; 18th c.
family notes.

Le Brune
See Browne

Le Heup
CULLUM, GERY MILNER GIBSON. 'Pedigree of
the family of Le Heup, *etc*: wills, *etc*',
M.G.H. 4th series **2**, 1908, 198-201 & 236-
40. London, Suffolk, *etc.,* 18th c. Includes
wills of Horatio Walpole of Woolterton,
Norfolk, 1748; Peter Lombard of
Westminster, Middlesex, 1720; William
Lowndes of Astwood Bury,
Buckinghamshire, 1767; and Lewis
Charles Montolieu of Westminster,
Middlesex, 1769. Also includes extracts
from registers of Hesset, Suffolk, and
Spitalfields.
'Pedigree of the Huguenot family of Le
Heup, together with those of Montolieu,
Lowndes-Stone, *etc.,* their descendants',
M.G.H. 4th series **2**, 1908, 114-8 & 157-63.
Of London, Suffolk, *etc.* 18-19th c.
See also Wittewronge

Le Keux
WAGNER, HENRY. 'The Huguenot refugee
family of Le Keux', *M.G.H.* N.S. **3**, 1880,
349-52. 18-19th c.

Le May
LE MAY, REGINALD. *Records of the Le
May family in England 1630-1950).*
Whitefriars Press, 1958. Includes pedigree,
17-20th c.

Le Strange
'Grant of the manor of Holborn, temp Ric.II, with some notes on the family of the grantor', *T.L.M.A.S.* **1**, 1860, 124-9. Includes pedigree of Le Strange, 14-15th c.

Leake
See Brown

Legay
BROWNBILL, J. 'Legay of Southampton and London', *Notes and queries* 12th series **8**, 1921, 341-3, 362-4 & 385-6. See also 451-2. 16-18th c.

Leman(n)
WAGNER, HENRY. 'Pedigree of Lemann', *M.G.H.* 4th series **5**, 1913, 175-6. 18-20th c.
WEINSTEIN, ROSEMARY. 'The making of a Lord Mayor, Sir John Leman (1544-1632): the integration of a stranger family', *Proceedings of the Huguenot Society of London* **24**, 1986, 316-24.

Lenthall
'Lenthall pedigree', *M.G.H.* 5th series **1**, 1916, 226. 17th c.

Leppington
See Skilbeck

Lethieullier
ELLIS, L.B. 'The Lethieullier family', *Pr.Hug.Soc.L.* **19**(2), 1954, 60-67. 16-19th c., includes pedigree.

Light
LIGHT, JOHN. 'C. & R. Light Ltd: cabinet makers of Shoreditch', *East London record* **10**, 1987, 2-7. Light family, 18-20th c.

Liron
WAGNER, HENRY. 'Pedigree of Liron', *Genealogist* N.S. **21**, 1905, 50-51. 18-19th c.

Lobb
LOBB, DOUGLAS H.V. 'The Lobb brothers: wood carvers to the aristocracy', *Genealogists' magazine* **23**, 1989-91, 252-6 & 285-9. Of Saltash and London, 17-18th c.

Long
COX, COLLEEN A. 'The Long family of Eastcote', *R.N.E.* April 1983, 20-24. Includes pedigree, 18-20th c.
'Huguenot ancestry of Long and Watkins', *M.G.H.* N.S. **3**, 1880, 397. 18-19th c.

Longden
LONGDEN, HENRY ISHAM. 'Pedigree of Longden', *M.G.H.* 3rd series **3**, 1900, 101-8. Of Gloucestershire, London, *etc.*, 17-19th c.

Lucadon
WAGNER, HENRY. 'Fragmentary pedigree of the Huguenot refugee family of Lucadon', *Genealogist* N.S. **27**, 1911, 230-1. See also **28**, 1912, 64. 18th c.

Lumley
See Hall and Saunders

Lymsey
'Lymsey pedigree', *M.G.H.* N.S. **2**, 1877, 310. Of Kent and Middlesex; 16th c.

Lyster
ATTFIELD, MARGARET. 'A music hall family', *Family tree magazine* **9**(9), 1993, 4-5. Lyster family, 19-20th c.

McIntosh
See Barefoot

Madox
See Brown

Magnus
SEBAG-MONTEFIORE, RUTH. *A family patchwork: five generations of an Anglo-Jewish family.* Weidenfeld and Nicolson, 1987. Magnus and Montefiore families; includes pedigrees, 17-20th c.

Mallinson
MACKIE, W. EUAN. *The Mallinson story 1877-1977.* William Mallinson & Derry Mott, 1977. History of a timber merchant's family business.

Manning
MANNING, PETER. 'A Stepney sailor's family', *C.A.* **8**, 1980, 9-13. Manning family, 19th c.

WATERS, HENRY F. 'Pedigree of Manning and allied families', *N.E.H.G.R.* **51,** 1897, 389(f). Folded pedigree, medieval-17th c.

Manton
NEAL, W.KEITH, & BACK, D.H.L. *The Mantons, gunmakers.* Herbert Jenkins, 1967. Supplement published Tisbury: Compton Press, 1978. Of Grantham and London; includes pedigree 17-19th c.

Maplett
CHAMBERLAIN, GEORGE WALTER. 'The ancestry of Mary Maplett, wife of Samuel Gorton of New England', *N.E.H.G.R.* **70** 1916, 115-8. Includes Maplett family wills and parish register extracts, 16-17th c.

Mapp
MORRIS, DEREK. 'Charles and Mary Mapp: a discontented life', *C.A.* **64,** 1994, 20-21. Brief note on their separation, 1774.

Markell
TOWEY, PETER. 'The Markells of Enfield', *Metropolitan* **15**(4), 1993, 136-7. 18-19th c.

Marshall
SHONFIELD, ZUZANNA. *The precariously privileged: a professional family in Victorian London.* Oxford University Press, 1987. Marshall family; also includes pedigree of Seaton, 19-20th c.

Marston
MARSTON, TED. 'The Marston family of Harefield, Middlesex', *H.F.H.S.M.* **26,** 1994, 15-17. 19-20th c.
See also Rea

Masse
WAGNER, HENRY. 'Pedigree of the Huguenot family of Masse', *Genealogist* N.S. **24,** 1908, 40-41. 17-18th c., female descent to Oliver.

Massey
TREHERNE, ALAN A. *The Massey family: watch, clock, chronometer and nautical instrument makers.* Newcastle under Lyme: Borough Museum, 1977. Exhibition catalogue, includes pedigree, 19th c. Of Newcastle under Lyme, Clerkenwell, *etc.*

Mawhood
REYNOLDS, ERNEST EDWIN. 'The Mawhoods of Smithfield and Finchley', *Biographical studies 1534-1829* **1,** 1951, 59-77. 18th c.

Medley
'Pedigree of the family of Medley', in PHILLIMORE, W.P.W., ed *The London & Middlesex notebook.* Elliot Stock, 1892. 16-17th c.

Menet
WAGNER, HENRY. 'A tentative pedigree of the Huguenot refugee family of Menet', *M.G.H.* 4th series **4,** 1911, 223-5. Of London, *etc.,* 18-19th c.

Mercer
BRAITHWAITE, MARION. 'The Mercer family of Uxbridge and West Drayton', *U.R.* **32,** 1979, 3-5. Includes pedigree, 18-20th c.
SWIFT, M.P. 'Some notes about the Mercer family of Uxbridge and West Drayton', *M.L.H.C.B.* **10,** 1968, 13-16. 18-20th c.

Messenger
REED, FRANCES. 'The Uxbridge Messengers', *W.M.* **6**(5), 1987, 135-8. 19th c., includes pedigree.

Middleton
PINK, WILLIAM DUNCOMBE. *Notes on the Middleton family of Denbighshire & London &c., with special reference to (1) Middleton of Cadwgan Hall, Wrexham 1891 (2) Middleton of Chirk Castle (Baronets) (3) Middleton of Ruthin and London (Baronets) &c., &c., &c.* Chester: Chester Courant, 1891. Medieval-19th c.

Milbourne
MILBOURN, THOMAS. 'The Milbourne alms-houses, and a brief account of the founder and his family', *T.L.M.A.S.* **3,** 1870, 138-52. Milbourne family, 16th c. The alms-houses were in Coopers Row.

Millett
EVANS, CHARLES. 'Millett, of Hayes, Middlesex', *Notes and queries* **208**; N.S. **10,** 1963, 403-5. 15-16th c.

Milligan
PARFITT, EVE. 'Looking for Milligan – do I mean Mulligan?', *C.A.* **2**, 1978, 3-7. 19th c.

Mills
THOMAS, DAVID W. 'The Mills family: London sugar merchants of the 18th century', *Business history* **11**, 1969, 3-10.

Minet
MINET, WILLIAM. *Some account of the Huguenot family of Minet, from their coming out of France at the revocation of the Edict of Nantes MDCLXXXVI ...* Spottiswoode & Co., 1892. Of Kent, London, etc., includes wills, monumental inscriptions and pedigrees.
WHITE, B.T. 'The Minet family and Hayes', *J.H.H.L.H.S.* **31**, 1985, 6-11. Includes pedigree, 17-20th c.

Mitton
See Dickens

Mobbs
The Mobbs claim to the Wenlock estates. [ ], 1866. Includes pedigree, 18-19th c., and will of John Mobbs of Islington, 1790.

Monk
MONK, D.G. 'The Monks of Monken Hadley', *N.M.* **5**(2), 1982/3, 37-9. Monk family, 18-19th c.

Monoux
DASHWOOD, G.H. 'Remarks on a deed of Sir George Monoux, Lord Mayor of London', *T.L.M.A.S.* **2**, 1864, 144-50. Includes pedigree of Monoux, 16th c., the deed relates to Boughton, Norfolk.

Montague
R., V. 'Bearers of the title, Viscount Sunbury', *J.S.S.L.H.S.* **4**, 1967, 13-17. Includes folded pedigree of Montague, 17-18th c.

Montefiore
See Magnus

Montrésor
WAGNER, HENRY. 'The Huguenot refugee family of Montrésor', *Pr.Hug.Soc.L.* **11**, 1915-17, 293-300. Folded pedigree, 17-19th c. Of London and Kent.

Moore
'Moore', *M.G.H.* N.S. **2**, 1877, 111. Of St.Botolph without Aldersgate; parish register extracts, 18th c.

Mordaunt
HARVEY, WILLIAM J. 'Mordaunt', *M.G.H.* 4th series **1**, 1906, 194-5. Extracts from family bible, 18th c.

More
HASTINGS, MARGARET. 'The ancestry of Sir Thomas More', *Gl.M.* **2**(2), 1961, 47-67. Includes pedigree, deeds and wills, 15-16th c.
MARSDEN-SMEDLEY, BASIL. 'The Lockey miniature of Sir Thomas More, his family, and some descendants', *Chelsea Society annual report* **1962**, 49-54. 16-17th c. *See also* Daunse

Morley
VAN DULKEN, S.C. 'Searching for Westminster Morleys', *W.M.* **3**(2), 1982, 34-5. 18-19th c.

Morphy
ALGER, BRENDAN. 'Mrs Morphy's family and Moorfields Chapel, 1770-1780', *L.R.* **8**, 1978, 39-41. Morphy family.

Morres
BLOOM, J. HARVEY. 'Genealogical notes: register of St.Martinin-the-Fields', *M.G.H.* 5th series **7**, 1929-31, 50. Extracts concerning Morres, Whealer and Sabine, 17-18th c.

Morton
TENISON, C.M. 'A London citizen's diary', *M.G.H.* 3rd series **4**, 1902, 176-8. Pedigree, etc., of Morton and Farrington families, of Devon and London, 17-18th c.

Moss
See Barefoot

Mower
See Nicholas

Mulligan
See Milligan

Murray
OSWELL, W.H. 'A Murray pedigree', *M.G.H.*
4th series **2**, 1908, 166-75. Of the United
States, London, *etc.,* 18-19th c.
WHITE, W. PHYLLIS. 'A Scots family, the
Murrays, in early Victorian Bow', *C.A.* **2**,
1979, 18-23. 19th c.

Myddelton
CULLUM, G. MILNER GIBSON. 'Myddelton
family', *M.G.H.* 3rd series **2**, 1898, 49-54 &
66-71. Of London, Denbighshire,
Northamptonshire and various other
counties; wills, 16-18th c., including some
of Dolben family.

Nansiglos
MORIARTY, G. ANDREWS. 'The Nansiglos
family', *M.G.H.* 5th series **5**, 1923-5, 38-46.
Includes pedigree, 14-16th c., wills, deeds,
etc.

Neal
GASKELL, MARTIN. *Harry Neal Ltd: a family
of builders.* Cambridge: Granta Editions,
1989. Includes pedigree of Neal, 18-20th c.,
of Ibstock, Leicestershire, and London.

Nelham
See Nicholas

Nicholas
JACOBS, DEREK. 'Some sixteenth century
Ruislip families', *R.N.E.,* April 1989, 7-17.
Includes pedigrees of Nicholas, Fearne,
Robyns, Winchester, Mower and Nelham,
and notes on Reading.

Nicholl
NICHOLS, F.M. 'An account of the family of
Nicholl, Nicholls, or Nicolls of London,
and of Ampthill, Co.Bedford, with notes
of their wills', *Topographer and
genealogist* **3**, 1858, 533-44. Pedigree, 16-
17th c.

Nind
SKELTON, HENRY ROUGHTON. 'The name of
Nind', *C.A.* **70**, 1996, 8-9. Of London,
Gloucestershire, *etc.*

Noël
NOËL, L., & SONS LTD *The centenary of a
family business 1860-1960.* Noël & Sons,
1960. Noël family business, 19-20th c.

Norris
DANIEL-TYSSEN, J.R. 'Norris pedigree',
M.G.H. N.S. **1**, 1874, 101-3. Of Somerset
and London, *etc.,* 16-19th c.

Nott
'Pedigree of Nott of London and Braydon,
Wilts.', *M.G.H.* N.S. **3**, 1880, 233-5.

Offley
BOWER, G.C. 'A manuscript relating to the
family of Offley', *Genealogist* N.S. **19**,
1903, 1-11, 83-8 & 149-53. Of Staffordshire
and London, 16th c.
BOWER, G.C., & HARWOOD, H.W.F. 'Pedigree of
Offley', *Genealogist* N.S. **19**, 1903, 217-31;
20, 1904, 49-56, 78-86, 197-9 & 268-74. Of
London, Staffordshire and Cheshire, 16-
19th c.

Ogier
STURMER, HERBERT HEATON. *Some Poitevin
protestants in London: notes about the
families of Ogier, from Sigournais, and
Creuze of Chatellerault and Niort.* The
author, 1896. 17-18th c.
EVANS, CHARLES. 'Ogier family', *N.E.H.G.R.*
121, 1967, 22931. 18-19th c.

Oldfield
GORTON, EDNA. 'An Islington family', *N.M.*
12, 1990, 127-30. Oldfield family, 18-19th c.
GORTON, EDNA. 'The Oldfield family of
Islington', *Islington history journal* **40**,
1994, 6-7. 18-19th c.

Oliver
SHERIDAN, RICHARD B. 'Planters and
merchants: the Oliver family of Antigua
and London, 1716-1884', *Business history*
13, 1971, 104-23.

Onslow
'Memoranda of births, marriages and deaths at the end of the Onslow family bible ...', *M.G.H.* 2nd series 1, 1886, 266-7. 18th c. *See also* Warner

Orleans
CASHMORE, T.H.R. *The Orleans family in Twickenham, 1800-1932.* B.T.L.H.S. paper 49, 1982. The French royal family. Includes pedigree.

Orten
See Hotton

Osborne
COKAYNE, G.E. 'Pedigrees of the families of Osborne and Buckby', *Genealogist* N.S. 24, 1908, 1-14. Of London and Bedfordshire; 16-18th c.

Ott
See James

Ouvry
OUVRY, JONATHAN GARNAULT. 'The Ouvry family in the 19th century', *Pr.Hug.Soc.L.* 24(6), 1988, 473-9.

Overbury
MARSHALL, G.W. 'The Overbury family', *Genealogist* 1, 1877, 267-70. See also 2, 1878, 364-5. Includes will of Sir Nicholas Overbury of Bourton on the Hill, Gloucestershire, 1640, with extracts from London parish registers, 16-17th c.

Oxley
HOVENDEN, ROBERT. 'Oxley', *M.G.H.* 3rd series 2, 1898, 74-6. Of Norfolk and London, *etc.,* from family bible, 18-19th c.

Palgrave
EDWARDS, LEWIS. 'A remarkable family: the Palgraves', in SHAFTESLEY, JOHN M., ed. *Remember the days: essays on Anglo-Jewish history presented to Cecil Roth* . . . Jewish Historical Society of England, 1966, 303-22. 19th c.

Palmer
BROWNBILL, J. 'Palmer of Little Chelsea', *Genealogists' magazine* 2(3), 1926, 67-72. Includes pedigree, 16-19th c.

Parker
PARKER, EDWARD MILWARD SEEDE. *Genealogical memoranda relating to the family of Parker, of Upton House, Upton Cheyney Manor, Bitton, Gloucestershire, and Welford House, Keynsham, Somerset; of Henbury, Clifton, Bristol, London and elsewhere, from 1543 to 1898.* Bristol: Lavars & Co., 1899.

Patient
PATIENT, JOHN. 'The Patients move to London', *C.A.* 72, 1996, 32-3. See also 73, 1997, 22-3. Patient family formerly of Great Easton, Essex, 19th c.

Patteshall
STONE, WILLIAM EBEN. 'Genealogical research in England: Patteshall', *N.E.H.G.R.* 72, 1918, 153-8. 16-18th c., includes extracts from St. Mary Le Strand parish registers, 1589-1667.

Peachey
GOLLAND, J.S. 'The Peachey stone', *Stanmore and Harrow Historical Society chronicle* 1980, 7-8. Peachey family, 17-19th c.

Peploe
See Browne

Pepperell
See Barefoot

Percival
HORWOOD, ALFRED J. 'The manuscripts of the Right Honourable the Earl of Egmont, at St.James Place', in Historical Manuscripts Commission. *Seventh report* . . . pt.1. C.2340. H.M.S.O., 1879, 232-49. See also *Seventeenth report* . . . Cd.3737. H.M.S.O., 1907, 143-53. Percival family correspondence, *etc.,* mainly 17-18th c.

Perrot
'Perrot', *M.G.H.* 3rd series 3, 1900, 13-17. Of London and Oxfordshire; 16-17th c.

Perry
PRICE, JACOB M. *Perry of London: a family and a firm on the seaborne frontier, 1615-1753.* Cambridge: Harvard University Press, 1992. Includes pedigrees; originally of Devon.

Petit

WAGNER, HENRY. 'Huguenot refugee family of Petit des Etans', *M.G.H.* N.S. **4**, 1884, 13-15. 18-19th c.

Pett

BURKE, H. FARNHAM, & BARRON, OSWALD. 'The builders of the Navy: a genealogy of the family of Pett', *Ancestor* **10**, July 1904, 147-77. See also **12**, Jan. 1905, 194-5. Of London, Kent and Essex, 16-17th c.

Petty

See Boddington

Phillimore

PHILLIMORE, W.P.W., & PHILLIMORE, LORD. *Genealogy of the family of Phillimore.* Devizes: George Simpson & Co., 1922. Medieval-20th c., includes pedigrees, *etc.*

Phillips

PHILLIPS, ELIZABETH. 'The Phillips family in Knightsbridge in the 19th century', *N.M.* **6**(4), 1984, 100-101.

Piacentini

GRIFFITHS, KAY. 'John Piacentini, Venetian glass silverer: runaway or legal?', *C.A.* **43**, 1989, 9-14. Piacentini family, 19th c.

Pike

PIKE, R.T. 'The Pike family tree', *W.M.* **7**(4), 1989, 141-3. Includes pedigree, 18-20th c.

Pilleau

CLAY, CHARLES TRAVIS. 'Notes on the ancestors and descendants of Pezé Pilleau, the London goldsmith', *Pr.Hug.Soc.L.* **16**, 1938-41, 338-68. 18-19th c.

Pinchbeck

KNOWLES-BROWN, F.H. 'The Pinchbecks', *Antiquarian horology* **1**, 1953-6, 26-8.
SHENTON, RITA. *Christopher Pinchbeck and his family.* Ashford: Brant Wright Associates, 1976. Includes pedigree, 17-18th c., wills, *etc.*

Pitman

PITMAN, H.A. 'Pitman: a family of London citizens', *M.G.H.* 5th series **8**, 1932-4, 168-71. Pedigree, 16-17th c.

Portales

WAGNER, HENRY. 'The Huguenot family of Portales', *Genealogist* N.S. **22**, 1906, 50-51. 17-19th c. Female descents through Wynantz, Dodd, Golightly, and Graham.

Powell

POWELL, EDGAR. *The pedigree of the family of Powell, sometime resident at Mildenhall, Barton Mills, and Hawstead in Co.Suffolk, and afterwards at Homerton and Clapton, Co.Middlesex, and elsewhere, from Henry VII to Victoria, to which are added pedigrees of Thistlethwayte of Co.Wilts.* The author, 1891.
See also Lawrence

Power

RYLANDS, J. PAUL. 'Power of Polesworth, Atherstone, Freasley, *etc.,* co.Warwick; Market Bosworth, co.Leicester; London, Dublin, *etc.*', *M.G.H.* 4th series **3**, 1910, 98-105. 18-20th c.

Previté

OLDAKER, JOHN. *A century of progress: the story of a family business 1859-1959.* Previté & Co., 1959. Previté and Co. Ltd., traders in asphalt; includes Previté pedigree, 19-20th c.

Price

KNOWLES, JOHN A. 'The Price family of glass painters', *Antiquaries journal* **33**, 1953, 184-92. 18th c.

Primrose

WAGNER, HENRY. 'Primrose', *M.G.H.* 3rd series **2**, 1898, 77-9. France and London, *etc.,* pedigree, 17-18th c.

Purdey

BEAUMONT, RICHARD. *Purdeys: the guns and the family.* Newton Abbot: David & Charles, 1984. Includes pedigree, 18-20th c.

Quinon

CORNELL, A. 'The Quinon family', *Honeslaw chronicle* **2**(2), 1979, 14-17. 19-20th c.

Radcliffe
DAVIS, RALPH. *Aleppo and Devonshire Square: English traders in the Levant in the 18th century.* Macmillan, 1967. Radcliffe family.

Raffles
GREEN, EVERARD. 'Pedigree of Sir Thomas Stamford Raffles, kt.', *M.G.H.* 4th series **2**, 1908, 154-6. 18-20th c.

Ragg
BURNBY, J.G.L. 'The Raggs of Edmonton Green', *Pharmaceutical historian: newsletter of the British Society for the History of Pharmacy* **5**(3), 1975, 2-3. 19-20th c.

Ramus
CLOTTU, OLIVER. 'The Ramuses of England', *Coat of arms* N.S., **5**(128), 1983/4. 226-31. 18-19th c.

Ravenor
KEENE, C.H. 'The Ravenor family in the Northolt records', *Local Historian [Ealing Local History Society]* **1**, 1962, 8-14. 16-18th c.

Ravenscroft
See Hall

Raymond
See Barker

Rea
HOVENDEN, R. 'Rea, Marston and Cope families: entries on a flyleaf of a book of common prayer', *M.G.H.* N.S. **3**, 1880, 31. 18th c.

Read
MURGATROYD, A.H. 'The Read family farm records', *W.H.S.J.* N.S., **3**, 1971, 59-70.

Reading
See Nicholas

Redman
UNDERWOOD, DAVID. 'The Redmans: cabinet makers of Shoreditch', *C.A.* **38**, 1988, 24-6. 19th c.

Reeves
LARPENT, F. de H. 'Reeves of Harrow School, 1745-1819', *Pedigree register* **3**, 1913-16, 33-5.

Rendel
LANE, MICHAEL R. *The Rendel connection: a dynasty of engineers.* Quiller Press, 1989. 19-20th c., originally of Devon.

Reneu
WAGNER, HENRY. 'Pedigree of the Huguenot family of Reneu', *M.G.H.* 4th series **1**, 1906, 313-4. 18th c.

Renouard
See James

Renvoize
BRADBROOKE, WILLIAM. 'The Renvoize (French Huguenot) family', *Genealogists' magazine* **2**(4), 1926, 98-102. 18-19th c.

Reyner
PEARCE, K.R. 'Reyner's the Chemists', *U.R.* **40**, 1983, 4-5. 19-20th c.

Rhodes
P., R.B. 'The Rhodes family in St.Pancras', *St.Pancras notes and queries,* 1903, 1-2 & 4. See also 9. 19th c., includes inscriptions.

Richardson
See Saunders

Rickards
'Rickards, Hadfield and Fremeaux pedigree notes', *M.G.H.* 2nd series **1**, 1886, 211-12. 17-19th c.

Rigaud
See Dutilh

Riou
WAGNER, HENRY. 'Pedigree of Riou', *M.G.H.* 3rd series **4**, 1902, 190-91. Of France and London; 18-19th c.

Riviere
RIVIERE, M.V.B. 'The Huguenot family of Riviere in England', *Pr.Hug.Soc.L.* **21**(3), 1968, 219-40. Includes list of paintings by members of the family, 18-19th c.

Rivington

RIVINGTON, SEPTIMUS. *The publishing house of Rivington.* Rivington Percival & Co., 1894. Includes pedigrees, 17-19th c., with inscriptions in St. Pauls Cathedral.

RIVINGTON, SEPTIMUS. *The publishing family of Rivington.* Rivingtons, 1919. 2nd ed. of *The publishing house of Rivington.* 18-19th c.

Roberdeau

WAGNER, HENRY. 'The Huguenot refugee family of Roberdeau', *M.G.H.* 5th series 1, 1916, 177-8. Pedigree, 18-19th c.

Roberts

GRIGSON, FRANCIS. 'Pedigree of Roberts of Willesden, Co.Middlesex', *Genealogist* 5, 1881, 300-307. 16-17th c.

POWELL, EDGAR. 'Roberts and Horde families', *Genealogist* N.S. 2, 1885, 46-7. Roberts of Willesden, Middlesex, and Horde of Ewell, Surrey; includes pedigree, 16th c.

VALENTINE, K.J. 'The Roberts family of Willesden', *T.L.M.A.S.* 36, 1985, 183-8. 15-18th c. Includes pedigree.

'Genealogical notes of the family of Roberts of Willesden, Middlesex, prefixed to a vellum ms. in the Bodleian Library ...', *M.G.H.* N.S. 3, 1880, 25-8. 16-17th c.

Robinett

LAYTON, W.E. 'Robinett and Scruby', *M.G.H.* 3rd series 4, 1902, 302. Extracts from parish registers, *etc.,* 16-17th c.

Robyns

See Nicholas

Roe

'Descent of Sir Thomas Roe, Kt., first husband of Mary, eldest daughter of Sir John Gresham, Kt., Lord Mayor of London, 1547', *M.G.H.* N.S. 4, 1884, 116. Medieval.

Romilly

ROMILLY, MIMI. 'Sir Samuel Romilly of Russell Square and his descendants', *C.H.R.* 20, 1996, 5-8. 18-20th c.

WAGNER, HENRY. 'Some Romilly notes', *Pr.Hug.Soc.L.* 8, 1905-8, 340-47. Includes folded pedigree, 17-19th c.

Rosell

See Barry

Rough

CHADBURN, REBECCA. 'The Rough family of Fulham', *W.M.* 3(3), 1982, 64-7. Mainly 18th c.

Roumieu

SPINK, KAREN. 'The Roumieus', *R.N.E.,* April 1993, 18-24. Includes pedigree, 17-20th c.

Rowe

ROBINSON, CHARLES J. 'Rowe family', *M.G.H.* 1, 1868, 166-8. Of Sussex and London; pedigree, 16-18th c., with wills.

Rowlet

BRADFORD, CHARLES ANGELL. 'Ralph Rowlet, goldsmith of London', *T.L.M.A.S.* N.S. 5, 1929, 85-114. Includes pedigree, 16th c.

Rumbold

RUMBOLD, HORACE, SIR. 'Notes on the history of the family of Rumbold in the seventeenth century', *Transactions of the Royal Historical Society* N.S. 6, 1892, 145-65.

Rushout

HEWLETT, GEOFFREY. 'The Rushouts and their family connections', *W.H.S.J.* 5(4), 1982, 69-74. Includes pedigree, 16-20th c.

Russell

RANSOME, DAVID R. 'Artisan dynasties in London and Westminster in the sixteenth century', *Gl.M.* 2(6), 1964, 236-47. Primarily concerned with the Russell family; includes pedigrees.

THOMSON, GLADYS SCOTT. *The Russells in Bloomsbury 1669-1771.* Jonathan Cape, 1940.

TRATEBAS, GLADYS N. 'Russell and Coates family of Cheltenham and London', *Journal of the Gloucestershire Family History Society* 38, 1988, 22-3. Includes pedigree, 19th c.

'Christening of a peer's daughter in the 16th century', *M.G.H.* 5th series 8, 1932-4, 179-81. Of Westminster; Russell family.

Rymer
ANSTRUTHER, GODFREY. 'The Rymer family', *L.R.* **4**, 1974, 347. 19th c.

Sabine
See Morres

Samborne
'Pedigree of Samborne, from visitation of London, 1687', *Genealogist* **1**, 1877, 218-9. Of Somerset and London; 16-18th c.

Samuel
HART, RONALD J. D'ARCY, ed. *The Samuel family of Liverpool and London, from 1755 onwards: a biographical and genealogical dictionary of the descendants of Emanuel Samuel.* Routledge and Kegan Paul, 1958. Includes pedigrees.

Sassoon
DOREE, STEPHEN. 'The Sassoons of Trent Park', *Heritage [E.H.H.S., Jewish Research Group]* **1**, 1982, unpaginated.

Satow
'A Clapton family in the 1850s', *The Terrier* **30**, 1993, 2-6. Satow family.

Saunders
HORTON-SMITH, L.G.H. 'Connection with ten City Livery companies', *Genealogical quarterly* **15**(4), 1948, 191-2 & **15**(5), 1949, 3-6. Notes on Saunders, Lumley, Golden, Say, Richardson, Baily, Smith and Horton-Smith, 17-20th c.

Savill
WATSON, JOHN A.F. *Savills: a family and a firm, 1652-1977.* Hutchinson Benham, 1977. Includes pedigree.

Say
HORTON-SMITH, LIONEL G.H. *The old City family of Say and its connection with Essex.* Colchester: Benham and Company, 1948. Reprinted from *Essex review.* 17-18th c.
See Saunders

Scarr
SCARR, JACK RENFORTH. *A history of the Scarr family.* Oxford: the author, 1993. of Wensleydale and Swaledale, Yorkshire, London, Bishop's Stortford, Hertfordshire, *etc.* 16-20th c.

Scrimshire
See Skilbeck

Scruby
See Robinett

Scruggs
DAVIS, WALTER GOODWIN. 'Genealogical research in England: Scruggs of Salem, Mass.', *N.E.H.G.R.* **85**, 1931, 388-95. Of London and Norfolk, 16-17th c., includes wills and parish register extracts.

Seaton
See Marshall

Seeley
EELEY, RALPH M. 'The English life of Robert Seeley', *N.E.H.G.R.* **116**, 1962, 159-65. Includes extracts from the parish register of St. Stephen, Coleman Street, 17th c.

Seignoret
WAGNER, HENRY. 'Huguenot refugee family of Seignoret', *M.G.H.* N.S. **4**, 1884, 321-2. 18th c.

Shaw
NUNN, H. 'Pedigree of Shaw of Barthomley and Lawton, co.Cestr., now of London and America', *M.G.H.* 2nd series **1**, 1886, 309-10. 17-19th c.

Sheivell
WAGNER, HENRY. 'A tentative pedigree of Sheivell', *M.G.H.* 4th series **4**, 1911, 8-10. 17-18th c.

Shenston
'The Shenston family', *Transactions of the Baptist Historical Society* **5**, 1916-17, 190-92. Brief note, 18-19th c.

Sheppard
[BODDINGTON, R.S.] *Pedigree of the family of Sheppard.* Mitchell and Hughes, 1883. 17-19th c.
See also Bodington

Shuttleworth
See Haydock

Sikes
'Sikes memoranda', *M.G.H.* N.S. 2, 1877, 423-6 & 457-9. 1718th c. extracts from a memorandum book.

Sim
See Churchill

Simonds
ETHERINGTON, PETER. 'Tracing a Jewish family in East London', *C.A.* 43, 1989, 17-21. Simonds family; includes pedigree, 19-20th c.

Skilbeck
DAWE, DONOVAN ARTHUR. *Skilbecks: dry salters, 1650-1950.* Skilbeck Brothers, 1950. Includes folded pedigrees of Skilbeck, 17-19th c., Bagnall and Leppington, 17-19th c., Scrimshire, 17-18th c. and Gouthit, 18-19th c.

Slater
See Brown

Smith
HUNT, ALFRED. 'A few notes concerning the founder of Lincoln Christ's Hospital (or the Old Blue Coat School)', *Associated Architectural Societies' reports and papers* 35(2), 1920, 24-36. Includes pedigree of Smith of London and Welton, Lincolnshire; 16-17th c.
'Pedigree of Smith of Westminster, and Dry Drayton, Co.Cambridge', *M.G.H.* N.S. 4, 1884, 61-4. 18-19th c.
'Smith pedigree', *M.G.H.* 2nd series 1, 1886, 171. 17th c.
See also Saunders

Soame
'Soame of Suffolk and London', *East Anglian* N.S. 3, 1889-90, 210-11. Pedigree, 17th c.

Sommers
BLOOM, J.H. 'Sommers family', *M.G.H.* 5th series 6, 1926-8, 147-9. Notes from family bible, 17th c.

Sotherne
SOTHERAN, CHARLES. 'Sotherne and Sotheron families', *M.G.H.* N.S. 1, 1874, 217-23. Of London and Yorkshire; includes pedigrees, 17-19th c., and grants of arms.

Sotheron
See Sotherne

Spielmann
SEBAG-MONTEFIORE, RUTH. 'From Poland to Paddington: the early history of the Spielmann family, 1828-1948', *Jewish historical studies* 32, 1990-2, 237-57.

Spooner
CHESTER, J.L. 'Genealogical memoranda relating to the family of Spooner', *M.G.H.* N.S. 1, 1874, 332. 17-18th c.

Stafford
STAFFORD, SAM. 'The Staffords of Studd Street: the story of an Islington watchmaking family', *Illustrated Islington history journal* 28, 1991, 6. Brief note, 19th c.

Stephenson
LHOAS, ANNE. 'The gas connection', *W.M.* 3(3), 1982, 72-6. Stephenson family, 19th c.

Stint
TYLER, J.C. 'Stint or Stynt', *M.G.H.* 5th series 6, 1926-8, 209-12. Of London and Surrey; pedigree, 16-18th c., with wills.

Stockwell
STOCKWELL, RON. 'Grandad was illegitimate', *Roots in the Forest: the journal of the Waltham Forest Family History Society* 6(9), 1994, 177-82. Stockwell family, late 19th c.

Stokes
S[CHOMBERG], A. 'Stokes', *M.G.H.* N.S. 3, 1880, 309. Of London and Wiltshire, *etc.,* extracts from family bible, *etc.,* 17-18th c.

Stowe
STOWE, C.E. 'The Stowes of London', *N.E.H.G.R.* 10, 1856, 121-6. See also 281-2. Mainly 16-17th c.

Strachey
ASKWITH, BETTY. *Two Victorian families.*
Chatto & Windus 1971. Strachey of
Lancaster Gate; Bercon of Lincoln.

Strengthfield
'The family of Strengthfield', *M.G.H.* 5th
series **5**, 1923-5, 134-6. Includes pedigree,
18th c.

Stynt
See Stint

Sullivan
See Brown

Tanqueray-Willaume
See Willaume

Tatham
'Memoranda relating to the Tatham family
...', *M.G.H.* 2nd series **4**, 1892, 156. From
family bible, 18-19th c.

Tattershall
See Fox

Taylor
MINOT, ROGER. 'The Taylors of Brentford',
W.M. **6**(3), 1986, 81-5. 19th c.

Tegetmeier
'Charles Darwin and the Tegetmeiers',
Hornsey Historical Society bulletin **34**,
1993, 10-12. Includes pedigree, 19-20th c.

Teissoniere
WAGNER, HENRY. 'Pedigree of the Huguenot
refugee family of Teissoniere, known as
Dayrolles', *M.G.H.* 3rd series **2**, 1898, 292-
3. Of France and London, *etc.,* 17-18th c.

Teulon
WAGNER, HENRY. 'Pedigree of the Huguenot
refugee family of Tuelon', *M.G.H.* 4th
series **2**, 1908, 202-5. 18-19th c.

Tew
TEW, ALAN. 'The Tews of Finchley (and
elsewhere)', *N.M.* **4**(1), 1981, 73-4. 19th c.

Thistlethwayte
See Powell

Thomas
BLORE, CHARLES B. *Dr. Thomas: his family
and the background of his times.*
Northampton: the author, 1982. Founder of
the Christadelphians; includes pedigree,
18-19th c.

Thornhill
See Beaufoy

Throckmorton
See Finch

Titford
TITFORD, JOHN, *et al. The Titford family,
1547-1947: come wind, come weather.*
Phillimore, 1989. Of Somerset,
Wiltshire, London, *etc.* Prize-winning
study.

Townsend
'Pedigree of the family of Townsend',
M.G.H. N.S. **4**, 1884, 125-31. 17-19th c.

Travers
WAGNER, HENRY. 'Huguenot refugee family
of Travers', *M.G.H.* 5th series **2**, 1916-17,
196-7. Of Stonehouse, Gloucestershire, and
London, *etc.,* 18-19th c.

Trevigar
WAGNER, HENRY. 'A Trevigar record',
Genealogist N.S. **30**, 1914, 187-9. Includes
pedigree, 18th c.

Tristram
TRUSTRAM, E.J. 'Pedigree of Tristram, *alias*
Trystam and Trustram', *M.G.H.* 5th series
1, 1916, 161-72. Of Hertfordshire, London,
etc., 13-19th c.

Trollope
STEBBINS, LUCY POATE, & STEBBINS,
RICHARD POATE. *The Trollopes: the
chronicle of a writing family* Secker &
Warburg, 1946. 19th c.

Troughton
'Troughton', *M.G.H.* 4th series **5**, 1913, 233-4.
17th c.

Trumbull
LEA, J.HENRY. 'Contributions to a Trumbull genealogy', *N.E.H.G.R.* **49,** 1895, 148-52, 322-32 & 417-26. Of Newcastle on Tyne and London, *etc.,* includes extracts from parish registers, probate records, marriage licences, *etc.,* 15-18th c.

Trustram
See Tristram

Tryon
'The Huguenot families in England, 1: the Tryons', *Ancestor* **2,** July 1902, 175-86. See also **4,** Jan 1903, 256-7. Of London, Essex and Northamptonshire.

Trystam
See Tristram

Tufnell
TUFNELL, ELLEN BERTHA. *The family of Tufnell, being some account of the Elizabethan Richard Tuffnayle and his descendants, with a chapter on the properties of Langleys, Nun Monkton, and the manor of Barnsbury.* Privately printed, 1924. Of Essex, Yorkshire, and Middlesex.

Turner
TURNER, SAMUEL BLOIS. *Turner genealogy.* Privately printed, 1884. Of Gloucester, Middlesex, Suffolk, *etc.* Includes pedigree, 17-19th c.
SCOTT, JOHN. *Legibus: a history of Clifford-Turner, 1900-80.* Hove: King, Thorne & Stace, 1980. Includes pedigrees of Turner, 18-20th c., and Vachell, 18-20th c., also list of London partners.

Twining
TWINING, STEPHEN H. *The house of Twining, 1706-1956, being a short history of the firm of R. Twining & Co. Ltd., tea and coffee merchants, 216, Strand, London, W.C.2.* R. Twining & Co., 1956.

Tymewell
'Tymewell Bible records', *N.E.H.G.R.* **108,** 1954, 229-30. 1718th c entries in family bible.

Upjohn
LIGHT, RICHARD. *Upjohn.* 2 vols. Michigan: privately printed, 1990. v.l. A study in ancestry, covering 14 generations and 450 years. v.2. Two early journals: the life and travels of James Upjohn, 1784; the ocean diary of William Upjohn, 1830. Of Shaftesbury, Dorset, London, the United States, *etc.*

Vachell
See Turner

Vanneck
LEWIS, R.W.M. 'The family of Vanneck', *Genealogists' magazine* **8,** 1938-9, 19-20. 18th c.

Vaughan
DUNCAN, LELAND LEWIS. 'Vaughan', *M.G.H.* 2nd series **4,** 1892, 86-8. Of Tipperary and London; 18th c.
VAUGHAN, ANTHONY. *The Vaughans: East End furniture makers: three hundred years of a London family.* Inner London Education Authority, 1984.

Vickery
LAWES, WINIFRED. 'John Vickery family', *Hampshire family historian* **11**(4) 1985, 211. Of Middlesex; 19th c. entries in a family bible.

Vincent
BODDINGTON, REGINALD STEWART. 'Vincent pedigree', *M.G.H.* N.S. **2,** 1877, 239-43. 17-19th c.

Visscher
EVANS, CHARLES. 'De Visscher: a family of London merchants', *Notes and queries* **203;** N.S. **5,** 1958, 313-5. 16-18th c.

Wadmore
LAING, JOHN GROSVENOR, ed. *The Wadmores of London: an inquiry as to their origin and genealogy, their pedigree, and several biographical sketches, together with many pedigrees of families connected with them since 1776.* Privately published, 1953. Duplicated typescript. Medieval-20th c., includes numerous pedigrees of related families.

Wake

'Wake: from the visitation of London, 1687', *M.G.H.* 3rd series **3**, 1900, 72. Pedigree, 17th c.

Waldo

H., E.H. 'Waldo notes', *M.G.H.* 2nd series **2**, 1888, 254. 18th c., includes pedigree.
SIBTHORP, CONINGSBY. 'Waldo and Chase families', *M.G.H.* N.S. **2**, 1877, 100-3. Includes parish register extracts, 16-18th c., and monumental inscriptions from All Hallows, Bread Street.

Walpole

SHORTER, AYLWARD. 'Horace Walpole's Catholic uncle', *Catholic ancestor* **3**(6), 1991, 224-9. Includes pedigree, 17-18th c.

Warner

GOODALE, ERNEST, SIR. *Weaving and the Warners, 1870-1970.* Leigh on Sea: F.Lewis, 1971. Includes pedigree, 18-20th c.
'Entries relating to the Warner, Knevett, Onslowe and Browne families in a ms. book of hours (fifteenth century) formerly belonging to the Duke of Buccleuch', *M.G.H.* 2nd series **4**, 1892, 90-91. 16th c.

Waterlow

DENNY, HENRY L.L., SIR. 'Notes on the ancestry of the Rt.Hon. Sir William A. Waterlow', *Genealogists' magazine* **5**, 1929-31, 146-8. Of Kent and London; 17-20th c.

Watkins

RICHARDSON, WM.H. 'Family register of the children of Sir David Watkins, Kt., temp. Car.I', *M.G.H.* N.S. **2**, 1877, 554-6. Of London and Chalfont St.Giles, Buckinghamshire; 17th c.
See also Long

Watts

'Isaac Watts' family bible', *Transactions of the Congregational Historical Society* **1**, 1901-4, 275-6. Of London and Southampton, late 17th c.

Webb

DANIEL-TYSSEN, J.R. 'Extracts from the parish registers of Hackney relating to the Webb family', *M.G.H.* N.S. **1**, 1874, 16-17. 16-18th c.

Webster

MACLEAN, BRUCE. 'The Webster family of clockmakers', *Antiquarian horology* **1**, 1953-6, 93-6 & 109-12.

Weightman

See Wightman

Weld

See Fox

Wells

HARFIELD, T.J. *Wells: a family history.* 2nd ed. The author, 1988. Of Shefford, Bedfordshire, London, Surrey, *etc.* Includes pedigree, 17-20th c.

West

PINHORN, MALCOLM. 'Who was John West's mother?', *Hampshire family historian* **17**(1) 1990, 73-8. See also **17**(3), 1990, 172-5 17th c.

Westray

R., L.J. 'A theatrical family', *M.G.H.* 5th series **9**, 1935-7, 289-91. Westray family, 18-19th c. Of London and the United States.

Whealer

See Morres

Whelan

HOVENDEN, ROBERT. 'Whelan family memoranda', *M.G.H.* 2nd series **2**, 1888, 72. Extracts from family prayer book, 18-19th c.

Wheler

MARSH, BOWER. 'The parentage of Sir William Wheler, Knight and baronet', *Genealogist* N.S. **25**, 1909, 209-15. 16-17th c.

Whiteman

See Wightman

Whiting

WHITING, J.R.S. 'The Whiting family', *Family history* 7(40/42); N.S. **16/18**, 1973, 3-8. Of Lincolnshire, Nottinghamshire and London, *etc.*, 15-20th c.

Whittington

WHITTINGTON, MICHAEL. *The Whittington story: from the three counties to the City.* Cirencester: the author, c.1988. Of Herefordshire, Gloucestershire, Worcestershire and London. Includes pedigree.

TIBBETTS, G.R. 'Lysons and the model merchant: new light on the family of Sir Richard Whittington, Mayor of London', *Genealogists magazine* **19**, 1977, 9-14. Of Gloucestershire and London, 14-15th c.

Wightman

I'ANSON, BRYAN. *Records of the Wightman (Whiteman or Weightman) family.* Privately printed, 1917. Of Suffolk, Leicestershire and London. Includes wills, extracts from parish registers, *etc.*, with pedigrees, medieval-20th c.

Wilde

SALMON, ALAN GALE. *The history of Wilde Sapte, 1785-1985, with some account of the Wilde family.* Trowbridge: Redwood Burn, 1985. Includes Wilde family pedigree, 19-20th c.

Wilkinson

'Wilkinson of Tottenham', *M.G.H.* 5th series **3**, 1918-19, 189-91. Includes pedigree, 18-20th c.

Willan

GRAY, J.D. ALLAN. 'The Willan and Boothby families at West Twyford', *Local historian [Ealing Local History Society]* **4**, 1964, 1-3. 18-19th c. Brief note only.

Willaume

WAGNER, HENRY. 'Pedigree of the Huguenot refugee families of Willaume and Tanqueray-Willaume', *M.G.H.* 4th series **3**, 1910, 92-5. Of Tingrith, Bedfordshire, London, *etc.*, 17-20th c.

Willoughby

BODDINGTON, REGINALD STEWART. 'Pedigree of the family of Willoughby', *Genealogist* **2**, 1878, 91-4. Of London and Wiltshire; 17th c.

Wilmer

FOSTER, CHARLES WILMER, & GREEN, JOSEPH J. *History of the Wilmer family, together with some account of its descendants.* Leeds: Goodall & Juddick, 1888. 15-19th c., includes pedigrees.

Wilshin

WAGNER, MARY. 'The Wilshin family', *H.F.H.S.M.* **28**, 1994, 17-21. 19-20th c.

Winch

BROOKING, VALERIE. 'The Winches of Shepperton', *J.S.S.L.H.S.* **30**, 1993, 11-13. 18-19th c., includes pedigree and extracts from parish register, monumental inscriptions, the census, *etc.*

Winchester

See Nicholas

Winkley

WINKLEY, WILLIAM. *Documents relating to the Winkley family.* Harrow Press, [1863]. Of Lancashire, Lincolnshire, Middlesex, and various other counties. Includes wills, parish register extracts, pedigrees, *etc.*, medieval-18th c. *Additional notes on the Winckley family* were subsequently published, c.1892.

Winn

See D'Hervart

Winter

See Brown

Wittewronge

CULLUM, GERY MILNER GIBSON. *Pedigree of Wittewronge of Ghent in Flanders, Stanton Barry (Bucks) and Rothamstead House (Herts), together with those of their descendants Lawes, Capper, Brooke, Gery, Le Heup and Cullum.* Mitchell Hughes & Clarke, 1905. Of London, Buckinghamshire and Hertfordshire, 15-19th c.

Wode

SMITH, J. CHALLENOR. 'John Wode, Speaker of the House of Commons, 1482-4', *Genealogist* N.S. **36**, 1920, 57-61. Of London and Sussex; includes pedigree, 14-15th c.

Wood

DANIEL-TYSSEN, J.R. 'Extracts from the parish registers of Hackney, relating to the Wood family', *M.G.H.* N.S. **1**, 1874, 25-7. 16-18th c.

WOOD, ELIZABETH. 'Some Wood family letters from Oxford, 16591719', *Oxoniensia* **51**, 1986, 105-38. Of Littleton, near Staines; includes biographical notes.

See also Cranmer

Woodd

Pedigrees and memorials of the family of Woodd, formerly of Shynewood, Salop, and Brize Norton, Oxfordshire, now of Conyngham Hall, Co.York, and Hampstead, Middlesex, extracted from the records of the College of Arms, London, 1875. Mitchell & Hughes, 1875. 15-19th c.

Worthington

DANIEL-TYSSEN, J.R. 'Worthington: extracts from the registers of St.John, Hackney, Middlesex', *M.G.H.* N.S. **1**, 1874, 152. 17-18th c.

Wroth

PAM, D.O. *Protestant gentlemen: the Wroths of Durants Arbour, Enfield, and Loughton, Essex.* Occasional paper N.S. **25**. E.H.H.S., 1973. 15-17th c.

Wyatt

JUPP, EDWARD BASIL. *Genealogical memoranda relating to Richard Wyatt of Hall Place, Shackleford, citizen and carpenter of London, with an account of the almshouses of his foundation at Godalming, under the care of the Company of Carpenters.* Cox & Wyman, [1870?] Includes pedigree, 17-18th c.

Wylde

PRIDEAUX, W.F. 'The Wyldes of Hampstead', *Hampstead annual* 1906-7, 139-41. Brief note, 15-17th c.

Wynantz

See Portales

Yardley

MORGAN, ERNEST. *Yardley of London, 1770-1935.* Yardley & Co., 1935. Business history with notes on the family.

THOMAS, EDWARD WYNNE. *The house of Yardley, 1770-1953.* Sylvan Press, 1953. History of a family business.

Yevele

HARVEY, JOHN H. *Henry Yevele.* Batsford, 1944. Includes pedigree, 14-15th c.

Family Name Index

IMPORTANT

This is an index to sections 1 to 5 only; it does *not* include the numerous family names listed in section 6. Since the latter are in alphabetical order, it would be superfluous to index them.

Place Name Index

Author Index